THE LITTLE
BLACK BOOK OF

PARIS

D1283277

*The Essential Guide to the
City of Light*

VESNA NESKOW

MAPS BY   D LINDROTH, INC.

ILLUSTRATED BY
KERREN BARBAS STECKLER

PETER PAUPER PRESS, INC.
WHITE PLAINS, NEW YORK

CONTENTS

INTRODUCTION

Paris conjures visions of sophistication, drama, and romance. The clichés abound, yet there's no denying the allure and beauty of the City of Light. Flamboyant and mysterious, Gothic and modern, refined and bawdy—Paris is all these, with room for both grandeur and coziness. It is a city imbued with history, a center of art, culture, and fashion, a cauldron of the intellectual avant-garde. But it is also a city of well-tended gardens, of cafés highly suited to people-watching, a feast of grand architectural splendors and small delights around every corner. And speaking of feasts, the food's not bad, either!

Paris is best seen on foot, walking up and down narrow passages and wide boulevards. With map in hand, it's hard to get lost. But what a treat it is to meander through the streets, taking in unexpected pleasures at nearly every step.

We encourage you to do just that: wander the streets as you visit the sites in this guidebook. There are so many extraordinary places in Paris that we've kept to our favorites, those exemplifying Paris as a center of style and re-invention, both historically and today. By exploring the city you'll discover what you love most.

Paris is divided into numbered sectors called *arrondissements*, postal codes by which Parisians identify locations. However, we've arranged this guidebook by clusters of neighborhoods, or quarters. (You will find that we have included the *arrondissements* within the specific addresses of sites.) The first seven chapters cover such clusters in central Paris, each with its own map. The eighth chapter highlights places on the city's outskirts, and the ninth chapter includes short excursions to spots near Paris. We've also included an overview map of the entire city inside the front cover and a public transportation map in the back.

Once you've explored Paris and been enchanted by its beauty and spirit, you can quote Humphrey Bogart when, in the movie *Casablanca*, he tells Ingrid Bergman, "We'll always have Paris."

GREAT VIEWS

For the best—and it's free!—sightseeing tour, walk along the Seine River. The views are spectacular. Be sure to look down at the walkways bordering the water: you'll see lovers kissing beneath the trees, students poring over books, fishermen patiently holding a line in the water, and the occasional beret-topped *grand-père* calmly feeding the pigeons.

You'll find other great views from atop the Eiffel Tower, the steps and terraces of Sacré-Coeur, the Georges restaurant on the roof of Beaubourg (Centre Georges Pompidou), the roof of the Institute of the Arab World, and, following in the footsteps of Quasimodo, the North Tower of Notre Dame.

For a river view, ride a tourist boat *(bateau-mouche)* along the Seine. **Bateaux-Mouches** depart from the Alma Bridge *(T. 01-42.25.96.10, www.bateaux-mouches.fr)*. **Bateaux Parisiens** depart from Port de la Bourdonnais, near the Eiffel Tower *(T. 08-25.01.01.01, www.bateaux parisiens.com)*. **Vedettes du Pont-Neuf** *(Square du Vert Galant, Paris 1st, T. 01-46.33.98.38, www.vedettes dupontneuf.com)* are open boats. Or catch the **Batobus** *(T. 08-25.05.01.01, www.batobus.com)*, public transportation on the river, at any of its eight stops between the Eiffel Tower and the Jardin des Plantes.

HOW TO USE THIS GUIDE

We have included a map for each neighborhood with color-coded numbers corresponding to the places mentioned in the text. **Red** symbols indicate **Places to See** (landmarks and arts & entertainment). **Blue** symbols indicate **Places to Eat & Drink** (restaurants, cafés, bars, and nightlife). **Orange** symbols indicate **Where to Shop**. **Green** symbols indicate **Where to Stay**. Some restaurants and shops are closed in August, so check before going.

Here are our keys for restaurant and hotel costs:

Restaurants

Cost of an appetizer and main course without drinks

(€)	Up to 25€
(€€)	25€-50€
(€€€)	50€-75€
(€€€€)	75€ and up

Hotels

Cost per night

(€)	Up to 150€
(€€)	150€-250€
(€€€)	250€-400€
(€€€€)	400€ and up

Abbreviations

M métro (subway) station

ALL ABOUT MONEY

Money changing

The currency in France is the euro (€). ATMs abound and most places take credit cards. Visa is commonly called "Carte Bleue." MasterCard is often referred to as "Eurocard." Exchange rates for cash or travelers' checks are best in banks, but some offer the service for clients only. Avoid changing money in airports, train stations, hotels, restaurants, and shops. You can try these places:

AMERICAN EXPRESS: 11 rue Scribe, 9th *(M: Opéra, exit rue Scribe, T. 01-47.42.72.24)*

CITIBANK: 1-5 rue Paul Cézanne, 8th *(M: St-Philippe-du-Roule, T. 01-70.75.50.00)*

COMPTOIR DE CHANGE OPÉRA: 9 rue Scribe, 9th *(M: Opéra, T. 01-47.42.20.96, www.ccopera.com)*

MULTICHANGE: 8 bd. Madeleine, 9th (and other locations) *(M: Madeleine, T. 01-49.24.96.62, www. multi-change.com)*

Tipping

A 15% service charge is added to all hotel and restaurant bills in France. But sometimes an additional tip is appropriate. A few extra euro-cents in a bar or café is fine; up to 10% in a restaurant if the waiter was particularly good. In hotels, tip 1€/bag for bellboys, 1€ for room service, 1€/day for housekeeping. For taxi drivers, tip 10%–15% on meter fares. In hair salons, give 10%–15% for any service.

Got cents?

Decimal points and commas are reversed from the U.S. system. So euros are separated from euro-cents *(centimes)* by a comma, and hundreds are separated from thousands by a period. On price tags, a € sign often replaces the decimal point (8,50€ = 8€50).

PUBLIC TRANSPORTATION

Getting to and from the Airport

Paris's two major airports are Roissy/Charles de Gaulle (CDG) and Orly. Flights from the U.S. generally go to CDG. Free shuttle buses marked "ADP" (Aéroports de Paris) connect the terminals and go to the Roissy RER (regional rapid-transit train/subway) station. The airport RER costs about 9€ one way.

Taxis into town cost about 50€ during off-hours, more at peak hours. Car and van services require reservations (17€–27€ per person). Aéroport Limousine Service *(T. 01-40.71.84.62)* is a fixed-fare car service. SuperShuttle

Paris *(T. 08-11.70.78.12, contact@supershuttle.fr; www.supershuttle.fr)* is a door-to-door minibus service. Paris Airport Shuttle is another car service *(T. 09-51.65.18.65, www.paris-airport-shuttle.com)*.

Non-reservation buses include the Air France Bus, about 15€ *(T. 08-92.35.08.20, recording in French and English)*, and RoissyBus, the RATP city bus, about 10€ *(T. 01-48.62.22.80, for more info: http://paris.anglo info.com/information/6/airtransfer.asp)*.

More information on getting into the city is available at:
www.cdgfacile.com
www.parisnet.com/airporttransfers.html
www.parisnet.com/airportshuttle.html
www.worldtravelguide.net/france/paris-roissy-charles-de-gaulle-airport
paris-cdg.worldairportguides.com

Métro, RER, SNCF, and Travel Passes
"Le Métro" is the subway. Individual Métro/bus tickets cost 1€70, and a book of 10 tickets *(carnet)* costs 13€30. Visitors' passes are also sold at Métro stations and online. Métro lines are identified by different numbers and colors. There is a fold-out Paris Métro map in the back of this book. The Métro runs daily from 5:30AM to 12:40AM. For more info: www.ratp.fr.

The **RER** is a system of commuter trains that transports people from the outskirts of Paris into the central city. Many of the stations overlap with the Métro stations and can be used interchangeably (tickets and passes are valid for both within the city). There are five different lines (A, B, C, D, and E), each with a different color. These are indicated on the map in the back of the book with slightly thicker lines than the Métro lines. In some cases, it might be quicker to use an RER train to get from one destination to another because there will be fewer stops in between than on the Métro train. The RER trains run daily from 5:30AM to 1:00AM.

There are five **SNCF** *(reservations & information: from U.S. 011-33-8-92.35.35.35, in France 08-92.35.35.35, open daily from about 4:30AM–1AM, www.sncf.com)* rail train stations that travel much further out of the city. These can be used for long-distance destinations and excursions. The station names appear in boldface type in the map at the back of the book, and the lines are a light gray color. You would use these for destinations featured in Chapter 9.

Paris Visite is a pass for 1, 2, 3, or 5 consecutive days of unlimited travel on the Métro or buses *(www.ratp.fr)*. Some passes are for Paris only; others include outskirts.

PHONE NUMBER, S'IL VOUS PLAÎT?

When calling Paris direct from the U.S., dial 011-33 then drop the initial 0 in the number. When dialing within France or within Paris, dial the number as it appears (with the initial 0).

SHOPPING

Opening hours: We have included specific store hours wherever possible in this guide. As a general rule, Paris shops are usually open Monday through Saturday from 10AM to 7PM. But there are exceptions. Some shops are open on Sundays. Markets and neighborhood stores may be closed on Mondays. Boutiques often close for lunch, and small shops close for vacation, usually in August.

Sales: By law, sales *(soldes)* are held twice a year in France, in January and July. In Paris they last a month. At other times of year, good deals are marked in stores as *promotions*.

Tax refunds: If you spend a minimum of 175€ in one store, you can get a tax refund *(détaxe)*. You must show your passport and fill out a form in the store. On leaving at the airport, go to the *bureau de détaxe* to get your forms stamped. Do this before going through passport control or baggage check-in: you may have to show your purchases. Back home, return the pink copy in the envelope provided; keep the other for your records. If traveling to other EU countries, get your forms stamped in the airport customs office of the last EU country you leave. It takes about three months to get the refund.

Duty-free shops: Best at airports. The duty-free shops around Opéra and Palais Royal aren't much of a deal.

Chain and discount stores: Fnac is a chain store great for books, CDs, and electronics. Paris's main discount chain stores are Prisunic and Monoprix.

SAY IT IN FRENCH

Although it's best to carry a phrase book, here are a few basic words and phrases to get you started.

Bonjour *(bohn-zhOOR)* Hello; good morning/day

Bon soir *(bohn sWAH)* Good evening

Au revoir *(oh-vwAR)* Good-bye

S'il vous plaît *(sill voo plEH)* Please

Je voudrais… *(zhuh voo-DRAY)* I would like …

Merci *(mare-sEE)* Thank you

Oui *(wEE)* Yes

Non *(nOH)* No

Où est… *(oo ay…)* Where is …

le métro *(luh meh-tRO)* subway

un carnet *(un car-nAY)* packet of 10 subway tickets

un billet *(un bee-yAY)* ticket

la rue *(lah rOO)* street

l'hôtel *(low-tEL)* hotel; house/mansion

le magasin *(magazEHN)* store

le grand magasin *(gran magazEHN)* department store

le restaurant *(restorON)* restaurant

Parlez-vous anglais? *(par-lay voo ohng-LAY)*
   Do you speak English?

Où sont les toilettes? *(oo sohn les twalET?)*
   Where is the bathroom?

Ça coûte combien? *(Sah koot kombee-EN?)*
   How much does that cost?

Madame *(mah-dAHM)* Ma'am; Mrs.

Mademoiselle *(mahd-mwa-zEL)* Miss

Monsieur *(muss-YUH)* Sir; Mr.

ETIQUETTE TIP

Whether it's "Bonjour," "Au revoir," "Merci," or "S'il vous plaît," it's rude to address someone without saying "Madame" or "Monsieur" after the address. On entering a shop, always first say, "Bonjour, Madame/Monsieur." If you enter a store with a man and a woman clerk, greet both with, "Bonjour, Madame, Monsieur." Even the surliest Parisian waiter will say hello! Just don't call him "garçon"—it means both "waiter" and "boy" and is considered rude. Better to say, "S'il vous plaît, Monsieur."

BOOKING TICKETS

You can buy theater and concert tickets at any **Fnac** *(one branch is at 74 ave. des Champs-Élysées, 8th, M: George V, T. 08-25.02.00.20, www.fnac.com; hours: M–Sa 10AM–11:45PM, Su 12PM–11:45PM)* or **Virgin Megastore** *(52–60 ave. des Champs-Élysées, 8th, M: Franklin D. Roosevelt, T. 01-49.53.50.00, www.virginmegastore.fr; hours: M–Sa 10AM–12AM, Su 12PM–12AM),* and also at **Carrousel du Louvre** *(99 rue de Rivoli, 1st, M: Concorde, T. 01-40.68.22.22; hours: daily 10AM–8PM).* Same-day, half-price tickets (commercial fare) sell at **Kiosque de la Madeleine** *(15 pl. de la Madeleine, 8th, M: Madeleine or Concorde, www.kiosquetheatre.com/kmad_guide.asp; hours: Tu–Sa 12:30PM–8PM, Su 12:30PM–4PM).* Most theaters are closed on Mondays. Magazines with local listings for arts and entertainment are available at newsstands—in French, every Wednesday: *Pariscope; L'Officiel des Spectacles,* and *Zurban;* in English, the webzine *Paris Voice (parisvoice.com).*

Paris Museum is a pass for 2, 4, or 6 consecutive days of unlimited visits to museums (permanent collections) and monuments. Kids under 18 enter most museums free; those 18 to 25 years old at reduced rates. See the following Web sites for more information:

www.museums-of-paris.com
www.conciergerie.com
www.discoverfrance.net

SEASONAL EVENTS

Winter-Spring:

Africolor, Nov.-mid-Dec., African music festival *(various venues in St-Denis, M: Basilique de St-Denis, T. 01-47.97.69.99, www.africolor.com)*

Printemps des Poètes, Mar., national poetry festival *(various venues, 6 rue du Tage, 13th, T. 01-53.80.08.00, www.printempsdespoetes.com)*

Summer:

French Tennis Open, May-June *(Stade Roland Garros, 2 ave. Gordon-Bennett, 16th, M: Porte d'Auteuil, T. 01-47.43.48.00, www.frenchopen.org, www.rolandgarros.com)*

Quinzaine des Réalisateurs, May-June, films from the Cannes Festival *(Forum des Images, Porte St-Eustache, Forum des Halles, 1st, M: Les Halles, T. 01-53.59.61.00, www.quinzaine-realisateurs.com)*

Paris Jazz Festival, June-July *(Parc Floral de Paris, Bois de Vincennes, 12th, M: Château de Vincennes, T. 01-48.76.83.01, 01-49.57.24.84, www.parisjazzfestival.fr, www.parcfloraldeparis.com)*

Gay Pride March, last Sat. in June *(Interassociative LGBT, 5 rue Perrée, 3rd, T. 01-72.70.39.22, www.inter-lgbt.org)*

Bastille Day, July 14, celebration of French Revolution, dancing at pl. de la Bastille on eve, parade in morning, fireworks at Champ de Mars at night

Paris-Plage, mid-July to mid-Aug., sandy beach along the Seine *(T. 01-49.52.42.63, www.paris.fr/parisplages)*

Tour de France, July, ends at Champs-Élysées *(T. 01-41.33.14.00, www.letour.fr)*

Autumn:

Villette Jazz Festival, early Sep. *(Parc de la Villette, 211 ave. Jean-Jaurès, 19th, M: Porte de Pantin, T. 01-40.03. 75.75, www.jazzalavillette.com)*

Nuit Blanche ("All-Nighter"), early Oct., galleries, museums, bars, clubs open all night *(www.paris.fr, nuitblanche.paris.fr)*

FIAC, end Oct., international art fair *(Louvre, Grand Palais, and other venues, T. 01-47.56.64.21, www.fiac. com)*

Fête du Beaujolais Nouveau, mid-Nov., new vintage, wine tastings throughout the city *(www.beaujolais gourmand.com)*

Festival d'Automne, mid-Sep.–late Dec., festival of contemporary theater, dance, and opera *(various venues, T. 01-53.45.17.00, www.festival-automne.com)*

PARIS'S TOP PICKS

TOP PICK!

Paris offers an abundance of one-of-a-kind attractions for visitors. Here are 11 of the top picks not to be missed!

chapter 1

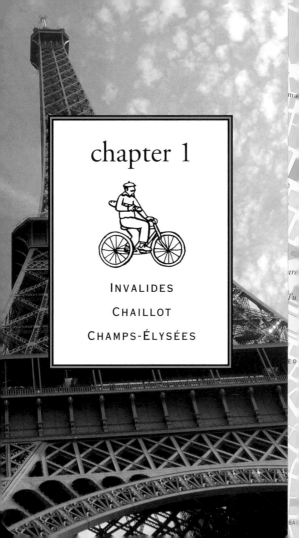

INVALIDES

CHAILLOT

CHAMPS-ÉLYSÉES

INVALIDES
CHAILLOT
CHAMPS-ÉLYSÉES

Places to See:

1. Pont Alexandre III
2. Hôtel des Invalides
3. Assemblée Nationale
4. Hôtel Matignon
5. EIFFEL TOWER ★
6. Rodin Museum
7. Sewers Museum
8. La Pagode
20. Palais de Chaillot
21. Trocadéro Gardens
22. Musée du Vin
23. Musée Guimet
24. Palais de Tokyo
25. Palais Galliéra Fashion Museum
26. Maison de Radio-France
35. ARC DE TRIOMPHE ★
36. Grand Palais
37. Petit Palais
38. Élysée Palace
39. PLACE DE LA CONCORDE ★
40. Atelier Renault
41. Théâtre des Champs-Élysées
42. L'Atelier des Chefs
43. Musée Jacquemart-André

Places to Eat & Drink:

9. Aux Ducs de Bourgogne
10. Bistrot le P'tit Troquet
11. Jules Verne
12. Café Constant
13. Les Fables de la Fontaine
14. Le Violon d'Ingres
15. Les Cocottes
27. L'Astrance
28. Les Echansons
29. Cristal Room Baccarat
30. Tokyo Eat
44. Café Jacquemart-André
45. Atelier Renault Café/Bar
46. Pierre Gagnaire
47. Restaurant Guy Savoy
48. Monte Carlo Restaurant Buffet
49. BE Boulangépicier
50. La Marée
51. L'Écluse François-1er
52. Nirvana

Where to Shop:

16. Maison Poujauran
31. Avenue Victor Hugo
53. D. Porthault

If you are lucky enough to have lived in Paris as a young man, then wherever you go for the rest of your life, it stays with you, for Paris is a moveable feast.

—*Ernest Hemingway*

INVALIDES

8 **13** to Invalides; **12** to Assemblée Nationale;
13 to Varenne; **8** to École Militaire;
6 to Bir Hakeim (Tour Eiffel)

• SNAPSHOT •

Over its colorful history, Invalides has been refuge to torn and tattered soldiers, a tool of rebellious crowds, and home to Napoleon's Tomb. From monuments to government buildings to 18th-century aristocratic town houses, the Invalides area exudes *hauteur* and beauty on a grand scale. It is the Left (southern) Bank's equivalent of Right (northern) Bank grandeur. It's home to the renowned Eiffel Tower, the magnificent Rodin Museum, and other "not-to-be-missed" sites.

PLACES TO SEE
Landmarks:

The Art Nouveau lamps of the ornate, exuberant **Pont Alexandre III (1)** *(off ave. du Maréchal-Gallieni, 8th)* create an elegant curve bridging the Seine River. The gilded statuary—cherubs, nymphs, and winged horses—of this flamboyant bridge leads directly to the **Hôtel des Invalides (2)** *(Esplanade des Invalides, 7th, 01-44.42.38.77/08-10.11.33.99, www.invalides.org; hours: Invalides tomb: Oct–Mar daily 7:30AM–7PM; Apr–Sep W–M 7:30AM–7PM, Tu til 9PM; Museum: Apr–Oct daily 10AM–6PM; Nov–Mar daily 10AM–5PM; closed 1st M of month, Jan 1, May 1, Dec 25)* on the Left

Bank. Commissioned by Louis XIV as a hospital for French soldiers, Invalides now houses several military museums, notably the **Musée de l'Armée** and **Napoleon's Tomb** (under the gilded Baroque dome). East of Invalides, along the Seine, is the **Assemblée Nationale (3)**, or Palais Bourbon *(33 quai d'Orsay, 7th, 01-40.63.60.00, www.assemblee-nationale.fr)*, the lower body of the French parliament. The Prime Minister resides at the **Hôtel Matignon (4)** *(57 rue de Varenne, 7th, closed to public)*.

On the other (west) side of Invalides is the **École Militaire** with its vast training ground, the **Champ de Mars** (great for jogging). At the far end of this park, bordering the Seine, is Paris's most renowned sight, the cast-iron

TOP PICK!

★**EIFFEL TOWER (5)** *(Champ de Mars, 7th, 01-44.11.23.23, 08-92.70.12.39, www.tour-eiffel.fr; hours: Sep–mid-Jun 9:30AM–11PM; mid-Jun–Aug 9AM–12AM)*. Built for the 1889 World's Fair and the centennial of the French Revolution, the *Tour Eiffel* was condemned in its time as an eyesore, called both a "belfry skeleton" and a "truly tragic street lamp." Guy de Maupassant said it was a "high and skinny pyramid of iron ladders...which just peters out into a ridiculous thin shape like a factory chimney." Some claimed they lunched there to avoid looking at it. Still, two million people visited the tower in 1889; less than a century later, it had become perhaps the most beloved symbol of Paris. Observation platforms at all three levels provide spectacular views, next to souvenir shops, cafés, and exhibitions. The stunning night view of Paris from the Eiffel Tower may leave you breathless; and for ten minutes every hour a dazzling 20,000-bulb light show makes the ironwork seem magical.

Arts & Entertainment:

The **Rodin Museum (6)** *(79 rue de Varenne, 7th, 01-44. 18.61.10, www.musee-rodin.fr; hours: 10AM–5:45PM; closed M)* is one of the best in Paris, with Auguste Rodin's great sculptures on display both inside and in the garden outside. Don't miss *The Kiss*, *The Thinker*, *Balzac*, *The Gates of Hell*, and *The Burghers of Calais*. For a unique underground museum, pop into the **Sewers Museum (7)** *(Musée des égouts de Paris, opposite 93 quai d'Orsay, off the Alma Bridge, 7th, 01-53.68.27.81, www.egouts.tenebres.eu; hours: Oct–Apr Sa–W 11AM– 4PM; May–Sep Sa–W 11AM–5PM)*. If you're in the mood for a non-mainstream film, **La Pagode (8)** *(57 bis, rue de Babylone, 7th, 01-45.55.48.48, www.etoile-cinemas. com/pagode; call for show times)* shows international independent films.

PLACES TO EAT & DRINK

Lunch at the cozy *crêperie* **Aux Ducs de Bourgogne (9)** (€) *(30 rue de Bourgogne, 7th, 01-45.51.32.48)* or order take-outs. The intimate **Bistrot le P'tit Troquet (10)** *(€– €€)* *(28 rue de l'Exposition, 7th, 08- 99.96.11.45, lepetittroquet.abemadi.com; M–Sa 12PM–2:30PM, 7:30PM–10:30PM)*

serves traditional French food. The food and the views at **Jules Verne (11)** (€€€€) (*Eiffel Tower, Level 2, 7th, 01-45.55. 61.44, www.lejulesverne-paris.com; hours: 12:15PM–1:30PM, 7PM–9:30PM, book ahead*) are fabulous, but the less expensive **Eiffel Tower (5)** cafés have the same vista. Chef Christian Constant boasts three restaurants in the area: **Café Constant (12)** (€) (*139 rue St-Dominique, 7th, 01-47.53.73.34, www. maisonconstant.com; hours: daily 12PM–2:30PM, 7PM–10:30PM, drinks all day*), **Les Fables de la Fontaine (13)** (€€) (*131 rue St-Dominique, 7th, 01-44.18.37.55, www.lesfablesdelafontaine.net; hours: 12:30PM–2:30PM, 7:30PM–10:30PM*) for seafood, and the exquisite **Le Violon d'Ingres (14)** (€€€) (*135 rue St-Dominique, 7th, 01-45.55.15.05, www.maisonconstant.com; hours: 12PM–2:30PM, 7PM–10:30PM*). Hugely hip **Les Cocottes (15)** (€–€€) (*135 rue Saint-Dominique, 7th, no reservations, www.maisonconstant.com; 12PM–3PM, 7PM–10:30PM*) is the French answer to the American diner.

WHERE TO SHOP

At **Maison Poujauran (16)** (*18-20 rue Jean-Nicot, 7th, 01-47.05.80.88*), a tiny old-fashioned *boulangerie*, you'll find wonderful *baguettes* and biscuits (*sablés*); it's the official bread supplier to the Élysée Palace, the presidential residence—credentials well-earned.

WHERE TO STAY

Practical, minimalist rooms make **Grand Hôtel Lévêque (17)** (€-€€) *(29 rue Cler, 7th, 01-47.05.49.15, www.hotel-leveque.com)* a low-budget favorite. For elegance and luxury in the diplomatic neighborhood around parliament, **Bourgogne & Montana (18)** (€€-€€€) *(3 rue de Bourgogne, 7th, 01-45.51.20.22, www.bourgogne-montana.com)* exudes tradition for a classy clientele. Quiet and hospitable, **Hôtel de Londres Eiffel (19)** (€€-€€€) *(1 rue Augereau, 7th, 01-45.51.63.02, www.londres-eiffel.com)* is tastefully outfitted.

CHAILLOT

6 **9** to Trocadéro; **9** to Iéna or Alma-Marceau;
2 to Victor Hugo; **1** **2** **6** to Ch. de Gaulle-Étoile

• SNAPSHOT •

"Opulent" and "staid" best describe the exclusive Chaillot quarter. The village of Chaillot was annexed into Paris and underwent surgery during the modernizations of Baron Haussmann, under Napoleon III, to become a neighborhood of grandeur for the *haute bourgeoisie*. It is arguably one of the best places in Paris to catch phenomenal views of the city and its treasures.

PLACES TO SEE
Landmarks:

Facing the Eiffel Tower, across the Seine past the Iéna Bridge, is the monumental **Palais de Chaillot (20)** *(17 pl. du Trocadéro, 16th)*. Its two curved neoclassical wings, harsh and cumbersome, provide great photo ops from the central terrace: a magnificent view of the river and the Eiffel Tower. The **Trocadéro Gardens (21)** *(16th)* sweep down from the terrace, around a long central pool of fountains bordered by statues.

Arts & Entertainment:

The **Palais de Chaillot (20)** *(see also above)* houses several museums: for architecture, the **Cité de l'Architecture et du Patrimoine** *(1 pl. du Trocadéro,*

16th, 01-58.51.52.00, www.citechaillot.fr; hours: M, W, F–Su 11AM–7PM, Th 11AM–9PM); for anthropology and archaeology, the **Musée de l'Homme** *(17 pl. du Trocadéro, 16th, 01-44.05.72.72, www.museedelhomme.fr; closed for renovation until 2014)*; and for French maritime history, the **Musée de la Marine** *(17 pl. du Trocadéro, 16th, 01-53.65.69.69, www.musee-marine.fr; hours: M, W–F 11AM–6PM, Sa–Su 11AM–7PM)*. For the history of winemaking (and tastings), visit the **Musée du Vin (22)** *(rue des Eaux, 16th, 01-45.25.63.26, www.museedu vinparis.com; hours: Tu–Su 10AM–6PM)*. The **Théâtre National de Chaillot** *(1 pl. du Trocadéro, 16th, 01-53.65.30.00, www.theatre-chaillot.fr)* in the **Palais de Chaillot (20)** *(see also page 28)* stages classics and some musicals. Nearby is the **Musée Guimet (23)** *(6 pl. d'Iéna, 16th, 01-56.52.53.00, www.guimet.fr; hours: W–M 10AM–6PM)*, one of the world's major museums of Asian art. The Neoclassical **Palais de Tokyo (24)** *(13 ave. du Président-Wilson, 16th, 01-81.97.35.88, www.palaisde tokyo.com; hours: W–M 12PM–12AM)* is notable for its stunningly redesigned interior. It houses the **Museum of Modern Art** in the east wing and the **Site de Création Contemporaine** in the west wing. Versatile, dynamic, and imaginative, the space morphs for each exhibit's needs. The café terrace affords a great view of the Seine. Paris fashion shows are by invitation only, but the **Palais Galliéra Fashion Museum (25)** *(Musée de la Mode et du Costume, Palais Galliéra, 10 ave. Pierre 1er de Serbie, 16th, 01-56.52.86.00, www.paris.fr/musees; hours: recently renovated, call for hours)* holds two or three French fashion exhibits per year. Free concerts at

Maison de Radio-France (26) *(116 ave. du Président-Kennedy, 16th, 01-56.40.22.22, www.radiofrance.fr; call for concert times)* feature classical music and well-known popular musicians.

PLACES TO EAT & DRINK
Where to Eat:

Celebrity chef Pascal Barbot's culinary creations at **L'Astrance (27)** (€€€-€€€€) *(4 rue Beethoven, 16th, 01-40.50.84.40; hours: Tu–F 12:15PM–1:15PM, 8:15PM–9:15PM)* are superb; it's tiny, so book months in advance. For an exotic lunch experience, **Les Echansons (28)** (€€-€€€) *(rue des Eaux, 16th, 01-45.25.63.26, www.musee duvinparis.com; hours: Tu–Sa 12PM–3PM, book ahead)*, in the 15th-century wine cellar of the **Musée du Vin (22)** *(see also page 29)*, offers specialties such as parmesan-crusted scallops and crème brûlée with fruit coulis, along with a free ticket to the museum. For a trip into surreal fantasy, the Philippe Starck-designed **Cristal Room Baccarat (29)** (€€€-€€€€) *(11 pl. des Étas-Unis, 16th, 01-40.22.11.10, www.baccarat.fr; hours: M–Sa 12:15PM–2:15PM, 7:30PM–10:15PM, reserve 1 month ahead)* is very hot. The décor reflects the eccentricity of the mansion's former owner, Marie-Laure de Noailles, friend of

Cocteau, Dalí, Man Ray, and Buñuel. Or opt for a sandwich at one of the many elegant cafés on the Place du Trocadéro. The postmodern **Tokyo Eat (30)** (€€) *(Palais de Tokyo, 13 ave.*

du Président-Wilson, 16th, 01-47.20.00.29, www.palais detokyo.com; hours: W–M 12PM–2AM), the restaurant at the Palais de Tokyo (24) *(see also page 29)*, is as much an artistic and aesthetically pleasing experience as it is a culinary one.

Bars & Nightlife:

This staid neighborhood isn't known for nightlife. But there's a cultural night scene at the Palais de Tokyo (24) *(see also page 29)*, where fabulous exhibits of international art are open until midnight.

WHERE TO SHOP

A host of fashion designers display their work in boutiques along Avenue Victor Hugo (31), among them **Apostrophe** *(5 ave. Victor Hugo, 16th, 01-45.01.66.91, www.apostrophe.fr)*. The style strength of this particular avenue can best be described in two words: conservative and classic.

WHERE TO STAY

This area is not very exciting for tourists; it is well suited for business travelers. For casual French chic, **Au Palais de Chaillot Hôtel (32)** (€) *(35 ave. Raymond Poincaré, 16th, 01-53.70.09.09, www.hotelpalaisdechaillot.com)* offers bang for the buck. Guests rave about **Jays Paris (33)** (€€€€) *(6 rue Copernic, 16th, 01-47.04.16.16, www.jays-paris.com)*, offering luxury and outstanding service in a boutique environment. Close to the Trocadero Métro, comfortable **Plaza Tour Eiffel (34)** (€€- €€€€) *(32 rue Greuze, 16th, 01-47.27.10.00, www. plazatoureiffel.com)* is sited in residential surrounds.

CHAMPS-ÉLYSÉES

① ② ⑥ *to Ch. de Gaulle-Étoile;*
① *to George V or FDR;* **⑨** *to Alma Marceau;*
① ⑬ *to Champs-Élysées-Clemenceau;*
① ⑧ ⑫ *to Concorde*

• SNAPSHOT •

The Champs-Élysées district and the Place Charles-de-Gaulle (or Place de l'Étoile) epitomize the spirit of the *grands boulevards*. Twelve wide avenues radiate from the rotary of l'Étoile ("star"), cutting a grandiose swath through majestic *fin-de-siècle* residences. Despite the infiltration of commercialism on Champs-Élysées Avenue, the quarter is among the city's most aristocratic—and among the most popular for tourists who wish to take in perhaps the most famous avenue of the city. But the area is not just a tourist spot—it hosts numerous events and spectacular displays of national pride on days such as Bastille Day and New Year's Eve.

PLACES TO SEE
Landmarks:

TOP
PICK!

In the center of Étoile, an island in a sea of moving vehicles, towers the **★ARC DE TRIOMPHE (35)** *(pl. Charles-de-Gaulle/Étoile, 8th, 01-55.37.73.77, www.arcdetriomphe paris.com; hours: Apr–Sep 10AM–11PM, Oct–Mar 10AM–10:30PM).* Commissioned by Napoleon, the enormous, 164-foot-tall structure was to be a triumphal gateway for the emperor's returning armies. Instead, in 1840, four years after the building's completion, Napoleon's ashes passed beneath the arch on the way to his tomb in Les Invalides. Victorious French soldiers finally marched through the arch at the end of WWI. Beneath it lies the Tomb of the Unknown Soldier. Once the focus of fashionable society, the **Avenue des Champs-Élysées** has lost much of its aristocratic cachet but remains Paris's most famous street. The **Grand Palais (36)** *(Porte A, 3 ave. Général-Eisenhower, 8th, 01-44.13.17.17, www.grand palais.fr; open during exhibitions only; call for hours)*, an imposing exhibition hall with a magnificent glass-roofed central atrium, mixes classical stonework with Art Nouveau ironwork, topped with galloping bronze horses. Architecturally similar, the **Petit Palais (37)** *(ave. Winston Churchill, 8th, 01-53.43.40.00, www.petit palais.paris.fr; hours: Tu–Su 10AM–6PM, Th until 8PM for temporary exhibitions)* exhibits the city's collection of French and Renaissance art. Its dome mirrors the Invalides cupola directly across the river. North of the Champs-Élysées, the beautiful **Élysée Palace (38)** *(55 rue du Faubourg-St-Honoré, 8th, closed to the public),* with its English gardens, is the official residence of the president of the Republic. At the eastern end of the Champs-Élysées, the **★PLACE DE LA CONCORDE (39)** *(8th),* with its beautiful fountains, was built in 1750 with a grand statue of Louis XV in the center. During the

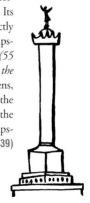

TOP PICK!

French Revolution, the statue was dismantled and a guillotine set up in its place: Louis XVI, Marie-Antoinette, Robespierre, and Danton, along with more than 1,000 others, all lost their heads here. Concorde, Paris's largest square, is a focal point for surrounding major landmarks: the **Arc de Triomphe (35)** (west) *(see also page 32)*, the **Madeleine church** (north), the **National Assembly** (south), and the **Tuileries Gardens** and **Louvre** (east). At the center of the square is a wonderful gift from Egypt—a 75-foot-tall **obelisk**, covered in hieroglyphics, from the temple of Luxor.

Arts & Entertainment:

Beside the museums mentioned earlier, it's fun to visit the **Atelier Renault (40)** *(53 ave. des Champs-Élysées, 8th, 08-11.88.28.11, www.atelier.renault.com; hours: Su–Th 10:30AM–11:30PM, F–Sa 10:30AM–1:30AM)*, where cars aren't only on the showroom floor, they're on the walls, too. The top classical music and opera concert venue is the **Théâtre des Champs-Élysées (41)** *(15 ave. Montaigne, 8th, 01-49.52.50.50, www.theatrechampselysees.fr; call for show times)*. Or take a cooking class at **L'Atelier des Chefs (42)** *(10 rue de Penthièvre, 8th, 01-53.30.05.82, www.atelierdeschefs.fr; hours: M–Sa 10AM–7PM, call for course times)* in a glass-roofed loft. **Musée Jacquemart-André (43)** *(158 bd. Haussmann, 8th, 01-45.62.11.59, www.musee-jacquemart-andre.com; hours: daily 10AM–6PM, M, Sa til 9PM during exhibitions)*, once the home of banker

Édouard André and portraitist Nélie Jacquemart, is an extravagant jewel containing an extraordinary collection of paintings, tapestries, and furniture.

PLACES TO EAT & DRINK
Where to Eat:

Café Jacquemart-André (44) (€-€€) *(158 bd. Haussmann, 8th, 01-45.62.11.59, www.musee-jacquemart-andre.com; hours: M–F 11:45AM–3PM, snacks daily 3PM–5:30PM, brunch Sa–Su 11AM–3PM)* is one of the most beautiful tea salons in Paris; check out the weekend brunch. The **Atelier Renault Café/Bar (45) (€-€€)** *(53 ave. des Champs-Élysées, 8th, 08-11.88.28.11, www.atelier.renault.com; hours: restaurant: daily 12PM–4PM; bar lounge: Su–Th 4PM–11PM, F–Sa 4PM–1AM) (see also page 34)* is a perfect people-watching place. An avant-garde, extravagant food experience for gourmets, **Pierre Gagnaire (46) (€€€)** *(Hôtel Balzac, 6 rue Balzac, 8th, 01-58.36.12.50, www.pierre-gagnaire.com; hours: M–F 12PM–1:30PM, 7:30PM–10PM, closed first 2 wks Aug)* dazzles as it delights. **Restaurant Guy Savoy (47) (€€€€)** *(18 rue Troyon, 17th, 01-43.80.40.61, www.guysavoy.com; hours: Tu–F 12PM–2PM, 7PM–10:30PM, Sa 7PM–10:30PM)* combines country inn hospitality with sensuous gastronomy. The cafeteria-style self-service at **Monte Carlo Restaurant Buffet (48) (€)** *(9 ave. de Wagram, 17th, 01-43.80.02.20/21, www.monte-carlo.fr; hours: daily 11AM–11PM)* is a great bargain for the area. It has many dishes to choose from and even comes with wine. Celebrity chef Alain Ducasse does gourmet sandwiches in his deli/bread shop **BE Boulangépicier (49)** (€) *(73 bd. de Courcelles, 8th, 01-46.22.20.20, www.boulangepicier.com; hours: M–Sa 7AM–8PM)*. Fish is the centerpiece at **La Marée (50)** (€€) *(258 rue du Faubourg St-Honoré at 1 rue Daru, 8th, 01-43.80.20.00, www.lamaree.fr; hours: 12PM–2:30PM, 7PM–11PM, booking preferred)*. Drugstore Publicis (58) (€€-€€€) *(133 ave. des Champs-Élysées, 8th, 01-44.43.77.64, www.publicisdrugstore.com; hours: M–F 8AM–2AM, Sa–Su 10AM–2AM)*, good for a quick bite, is a stylish general store with restaurants and a pharmacy.

Bars & Nightlife:

With a wide selection of wines to sample, along with seasonal French dishes, **L'Écluse François-1er (51)** *(64 rue François 1er, 8th, 01-47.20.77.09, www.lecluse baravin.com; hours: 8:30AM–1AM)* is a trendy wine bar. There's a line to get into the hip club **Nirvana (52)** *(3 ave. Matignon, 8th, 01-53.89.18.91; hours: open til 6AM)*, but it's friendly, and the dance floor rocks (the restaurant is expensive).

WHERE TO SHOP

In and around the triangle of **avenues George V, Champs-Élysées**, and **Montaigne** is an embarrassment of riches, overflowing with designer fashion houses. You'll find fine French linens at D. Porthault (53) *(50 ave. Montaigne, 8th, 01-47.20.75.25, www.dporthault.com)*. For specialty foodstuffs, Fouquet (54) *(22 rue François 1er, 8th, 01-47.23.30.36, www.fouquet.fr; hours: M–Sa 10AM–7:20PM)* is a dream. Fabulous white linen and stretchy laces are elegant and comfortable at Anne Fontaine (55) *(17 rue François 1er, 8th, 01-40.73.78.01, www.annefontaine.com)*.

Men's shirts and neckties are the focus at Alain Figaret (56) *(14 bis rue Marbeuf, 8th, 01-47.23.35.49 www. alain-figaret.fr; hours: M–Sa 10AM–7PM)*. Classic French high fashion can't get much finer than at Hermès (57) *(42 ave. George V, 8th, 01-47.20.48.51, www.hermes.com; hours: M–Sa 10:30AM–6:30PM)*. There's everything from toys to books to shampoo at Drugstore Publicis (58) *(133 ave. des Champs-Élysées, 8th, 01-44.43.75.07, www. publicisdrugstore.com; hours: M–F 8AM–2AM, Sa–Su 10AM–2AM)*. The chain store Monoprix (59) *(branch at 52 ave. des Champs-Élysées, 8th, 01-53.77.65.65, www. monoprix.fr; hours: M–Sa 9AM–12AM)* has a variety of good inexpensive items. Next door the Virgin Megastore (60) *(52-60 ave. des Champs-Élysées, 8th, 01-49.53. 50.00, www.virginmegastore.fr; hours: M–Sa 10AM– 12AM, Su 12PM–12AM)* sells CDs, books, and electronics.

Expensive art and antiques galleries line **Avenue Matignon**, as well as a stamp and postcard collectors' market. **Artcurial (61)** (*7 rond-point des Champs-Élysées, 8th, 01-42.99.20.20, www.artcurial.com; hours: M–F 10AM–7PM, Sa 11AM–7PM*) boasts one of the largest collections of art books in Paris. It auctions everything from classic cars to modern art and jewelry. The **rue du Faubourg St-Honoré** (and its continuation rue St-Honoré) is Paris's most famous street for shopping.

Prêt-à-porter designer shops abound, along with places such as the **Spa Le Bristol (62)** (*Hôtel Le Bristol, 112 rue du Faubourg St-Honoré, 8th, 01-53.43.41.67, www.hotel-bristol.com; hours: daily 9AM–9PM*) day spa and **Anna Lowe (63)** (*104 rue du Faubourg St-Honoré, 8th, www.annalowe.com; hours: M–Sa 10AM–7PM*), which offers savings of about 40% on off-the-runway women's designer clothes. Down the street, legendary **Roger Vivier (64)** (*29 rue du Faubourg St-Honoré, 8th, 01-53.43.00.85, www.roger vivier.com; hours: M–Sa 11AM– 7PM*) shoes are like foot sculpture from the inventor of stiletto heels.

WHERE TO STAY

Luxurious **Hôtel Plaza Athénée (65)** (€€€€) (*25 ave. Montaigne, 8th, 01-53.67.66.65, www.plaza-athenee-paris.com*) is a legend, drawing fashionistas, honeymooners, and aristocracy alike. The near-antiques at **Hôtel Résidence Lord Byron (66)** (€–€€) (*5 rue Chateaubriand, 8th, 01-43.59.89.98, www.hotel-lordbyron.fr*) lend a warm ambience while the courtyard soothes the senses. **Galileo Hôtel (67)** (€) *(54 rue Galilée, 8th, 01-47.20.66.06, www.galileo-paris-hotel.com)* is elegant and sophisticated, modest and quiet. Luxurious yet minimalist, **L'Hôtel de Sers (68)** (€€€) *(41 ave. Pierre 1er de Serbie, 8th, 01-53.23.75.75, www. hoteldesers.com)* was once a noble-man's *pied-à-terre*.

chapter 2

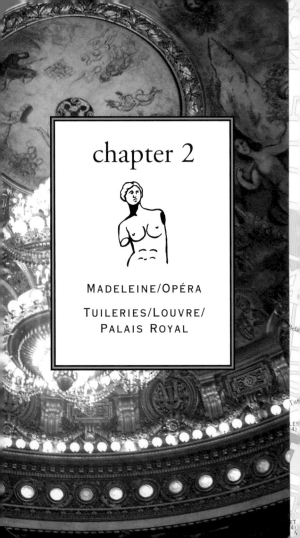

MADELEINE/OPÉRA

TUILERIES/LOUVRE/
PALAIS ROYAL

MADELEINE/OPÉRA TUILERIES/LOUVRE/ PALAIS ROYAL

Places to See:
1. Madeleine
2. OPÉRA GARNIER ★
3. Musée Gustave Moreau
27. Tuileries Gardens
28. Arc de Triomphe du Carrousel
29. LOUVRE MUSEUM ★
30. Louvre Pyramid
31. Place Vendôme
32. Palais-Royal
33. Galerie Vivienne
34. Galerie Colbert
35. Place des Victoires
36. Jeu de Paume
37. Orangerie
38. Museum of Decorative Arts
39. Comédie Française
40. National Library-Richelieu Branch
41. Legrand Filles et Fils

Places to Eat & Drink:
4. Café de la Paix
5. Fauchon
6. Hédiard
7. Senderens

8. Farnesina
9. Ladurée
10. Cojean
11. Chez Jean
12. La Patata
13. Harry's New York Bar
42. L'Ardoise
43. Ferdi
44. Le Soufflé
45. Lescure
46. L'Écume St-Honoré
47. Le Pain Quotidien
48. Le Carré des Feuillants
49. Angelina
50. Café Marly
51. Le Grand Véfour
52. L'Épi d'Or
53. A Priori Thé
54. Chez Georges
55. Café Moderne
56. Aux Lyonnais
57. Bar Vendôme
58. Le Café des Initiés
59. Le Fumoir

Where to Shop:
14. Maille
15. Jadis et Gourmande

★ *Top Picks*

41

Where to Stay:

MADELEINE/OPÉRA

1 **8** **12** *to Concorde;* **8** **12** **14** *to Madeleine;*
3 **7** **8** *to Opéra;* **7** **9** *to Chaussée d'Antin*

• SNAPSHOT •

In the 19th century Baron Haussmann transformed Paris from a medieval fortress village into a modern city. With extraordinary vision he created wide, open boulevards that gave the city its aura of splendor and assured its place as one of the most beautiful cities of the world. Besides increasing ventilation and integrating the newly extended water and sewer systems, the avenues had the advantage of making it harder for rebellious citizens to erect barricades—a lesson learned from the revolutions which took place between 1789 and 1848. Nowhere is his extraordinary urban planning as visible as in the areas around Madeleine and the Opéra. The opulent use of space, in boulevards as well as buildings, has made it a prestigious location for the headquarters of major banks, while its bustling streets attract tourists, fashionistas, and people-watchers.

PLACES TO SEE
Landmarks:

North of the **Place de la Concorde** at the other end of rue Royale is the Neoclassical church known as Madeleine **(1)** *(pl. de la Madeleine, 8th, 01-44.51.69.00, www. eglise-lamadeleine.com; hours: daily 9:30AM–7PM).* With its 52 Corinthian columns, it looks like a Greek temple. It faces what could be its mirror-image, the **National Assembly**, straight across Concorde and over the river. **Place de la Madeleine** is known for luxury food shops, but it was also home to luminaries: No. 9, for example, was

TOP PICK!

Marcel Proust's childhood house. Follow the majestic Boulevard des Capucines, and you'll arrive at the ★OPÉRA GARNIER (2) *(pl. de l'Opéra, 9th, 08-92.89.90.90, from U.S. 011-33-1-71.25.24.23, www.operadeparis.fr; hours: daily 10AM–5PM, mid-Jul to early Sep until 6PM; box office hours: daily 11:30AM–6:30PM; box office phone hours: M–F 9AM–6PM, Sa 9AM–1PM)*. Tons of gilt and marble went into building the **Paris Opéra**. Its mix of styles, ranging from Classical to Baroque, features gold busts, winged angels, rearing horses, and ornate columns. The façade sculpture *La Danse* by Jean Baptiste Carpeaux was deemed so shockingly suggestive it was once splashed with ink. Inside, the auditorium has a false ceiling created by Marc Chagall in 1964. Named after its architect, Charles Garnier, the opera house is emblematic of Second Empire grandeur and excess. Garnier also built the sumptuous **Café de la Paix (4)** *(see also page 45)* on the corner of the Place de l'Opéra and Boulevard des Capucines.

Arts & Entertainment:

The **ballet company** of the **Opéra Garnier (2)** *(pl. de l'Opéra, 9th, 08-92.89.90.90, www.operadeparis.fr; box office hours: daily 11:30AM–6:30PM; box office phone hours: M–F 9AM–6PM, Sa 9AM–1PM)* performs classical and contemporary pieces. The Opéra also hosts modern dance companies from around the world. The wonderful **Musée Gustave Moreau (3)** *(14 rue de la Rochefoucauld, 9th, 01-*

48.74.38.50, www.musee-moreau.fr; hours: M, W–Th
10AM–12:45PM, 2PM–5:15PM, F–Su 10AM–5:15PM) is
devoted to this Symbolist painter's art, life, and obsessions.

PLACES TO EAT & DRINK
Where to Eat:
If you're at the Opéra, the **Café de la Paix (4)** (€€€-€€€€)
(5 pl. de l'Opéra, Grand Hôtel Inter-Continental, 12 bd.
des Capucines, 9th, 01-40.07.36.36, www.cafedelapaix.fr;
hours: daily 12PM–3PM, 6PM–11:30PM, terrace daily
7AM–12:30AM) is an experience, if not for a meal, then
at least a café exprès and a sandwich on the terrace. The
saying goes that if you sit there long enough, you'll see
all the world go by. **Place de la Madeleine** is a cornucopia
of restaurants and luxury groceries. **Fauchon (5)** (€€-€€€)
(24-26 pl. de la Madeleine, 8th, 01-70.39.38.39,
www.fauchon.com; hours: café daily 8AM–12AM, deli
M–Sa 8AM–8PM) is famous for its fabulous delicacies, as
is **Hédiard (6)** (€€-€€€) (21 pl. de la Madeleine, 8th, 01-
43.12.88.99, www.hediard.fr; hours: M–F 12PM–
2:30PM, 7PM–10:30PM, tea 2:30PM–7PM, Sa 12PM–3PM,
7PM–11PM, tea 3PM–7PM); eat there or take it home.
Senderens (7) (€€€-€€€€) (9 pl. de la Madeleine, 8th, 01-
42.65.22.90, www.senderens.fr; hours: 12PM–2:45PM,
7:30PM–11PM, book ahead), in its Art Nouveau décor,
serves divine dishes; the prix-fixe lunch will burn a
smaller hole in your pocket. Isabelle Adjani and Inès de
la Fressange swear by the fantastic Italian fare at
Farnesina (8) (€€-€€€) (9 rue Boissy d'Anglas, 8th,
01-42.66.65.57, www.farnesina.fr; hours: M–Sa
12:30PM–2:30PM, 7:30PM–10:30PM). One of the most

classic tearooms in Paris, **Ladurée (9)** (€-€€) (*16 rue Royale, 8th, 01-42.60.21.79, www.laduree.fr; hours: M–Th 8AM–7:30PM, F–Sa 8AM–8PM, Su 10AM–7PM*) began as a bakery and sweet shop in 1862. Healthy soups, salads, and sandwiches at **Cojean (10)** (€) (*4-6 rue de Sèze, 9th, 01-40.06.08.80, www.cojean.fr; hours: M–F 8:30AM–6PM, Sa 10AM–7PM*) feature the freshest produce.

Chez Jean (11) (€€) (*8 rue St-Lazare, 9th, 01-48.78.62.73, www.restaurantjean.fr; hours: daily 12PM–2:30PM, 7:30PM–10PM*), with the fresh seasonal creations of its capable chef, is a bargain for nouvelle cuisine. For a cheap eat, **La Patata (12)** (€) (*25 bd. des Italiens, 2nd, 01-42.68.16.66, www.patatacafe.com; hours: daily 12PM–12AM*) offers salads and baked potatoes with a variety of toppings.

Bars & Nightlife:

Café de la Paix (4) (*see also "Places to Eat & Drink," open to 1AM*), is great for a relaxed people-watching evening. Ever classic, **Harry's New York Bar (13)** (*5 rue Daunou, 2nd, 01-42.61.71.14, www.harrys-bar.fr; hours: cocktail bar Su–Th 12PM–2AM, F–Sa 12PM–3AM, piano bar M–Th 10PM–2AM, F–Sa 10PM–3AM*) is still popular with American ex-pats in Paris.

WHERE TO SHOP

Place de la Madeleine is known for luxury foodstuffs: **Fauchon (5)** and **Hédiard (6)** (*see also page 45*) are practically unbeatable. On the opposite side of the square, Maille (14) (*6 pl. de la Madeleine, 8th, 01-40.15.06.00,* www.maille.com; hours: M–Sa 10AM–7PM), the famous mustard maker, sells divine mustards, vinegars, and olive oil. The specialty shop Jadis et Gourmande (15) (27 rue Boissy d'Anglas, 8th, 01-42.65.23.23, www.jadiset gourmande.fr; hours: M 10:30AM–2PM, 3PM–7PM, Tu–F 10:30AM–7PM, Sa 10:30AM–1PM, 2PM–7PM) is known for the tresse, a chocolate with nuts and candied orange peel. To satisfy a craving for a perfect piece of oh-so-slightly bitter chocolate, visit La Maison du Chocolat (16) (8 bd. de la Madeleine, 9th, 01-47.42.86.52, www.lamaisondu chocolat.com; hours: M–Sa 10AM–7:30PM).

Pamper yourself at the beauty salon Institut Carita (17) (11 rue du Faubourg-St-Honoré, 8th, 01-44.94.11.11, www.maisondebeautecarita.fr; Tu–Sa 10AM–6:30PM, boutique M–Sa 10AM–6:30PM). Eyeglasses have been the specialty of Lafont et Fils (18) (11 rue Vignon, 8th, 01-47.42.25.93, www.lafont-paris.com; hours: M–Sa 10AM–7PM) for three generations—conservative or eccentric, they make a fashion statement.

The **Place de l'Opéra** is encircled by specialty boutiques, like Lancel (19) (8 pl. de l'Opera, 9th, 01-47.42.37.29, www.lancel.com; hours: daily 10AM–8PM) for leather goods and **Clerc** jewelers. Behind the Opéra on **Blvd. Haussmann** are two of Paris's most renowned department stores: Galeries Lafayette (20) (40 bd. Haussmann, 9th, 01-42.82.34.56, www.galerieslafayette.com; hours: M–Sa 9:30AM–8PM, Th to 9PM) and Au Printemps (21) (64 bd. Haussmann, 9th, 01-42.82.50.00, www.printemps.com; hours: M–Sa 9:35AM–8PM, Th to 10PM), which carry designer ready-to-wear, among other things. Several streets north, L'Atelier du Chocolat de Bayonne (22) *(107-109 rue St-Lazare, Passage du Havre, 9th, 01-40.16.09.13, www.atelierduchocolat.fr; hours: M–Sa 10AM–7:30PM, Th to 8:30PM)* is famous for its chocolate bouquets. Adorn yourself with jewelry from Cartier (23) *(13 rue de la Paix, 2nd, 01-58.18.23.00, www.cartier.com)*. Thierry Mugler (24) *(49 ave. de l'Opéra, 2nd, 01-53.05.25.80, www.mugler.com)* is one of the designer's many fashion and fragrance boutiques.

WHERE TO STAY

A feng shui expert helped design the Zen-inspired Hôtel de Noailles (25) *(€€-€€€) (9 rue de la Michodière, 2nd, 01-47.42.92.90, www.hotelnoailles.com)*. Luxury in a modern setting makes Park Hyatt Paris-Vendôme (26) *(€€€€) (5 rue de la Paix, 2nd, 01-58.71.12.34, www.paris.vendome.hyatt.com)* the destination for elegant but trendy travelers with deep pockets; the glass conservatory-dining room, with its potted orchids and displays of works by contemporary artists such as Ed Paschke and Llyn Foulkes, is especially pleasing.

TUILERIES/LOUVRE/
PALAIS ROYAL

1 **8** **12** *to Concorde;* **1** *to Tuileries, Palais Royal (Musée du Louvre), or Louvre/Rivoli;* **3** *to Bourse*

• SNAPSHOT •

The Louvre, the geographic center of Paris, was built as a fortress against the English in 1190. Around 1360 it was transformed into a royal residence, undergoing alterations by successive rulers over the centuries. In 1793 after the French Revolution it was turned into a museum with the royal collection on public display. It remains one of the major museums in the world, with a vast collection of art and antiquities. Stretching between the Louvre and Concorde, the Tuileries Gardens are an extension of the Louvre, with pavilions on either side housing other museums. Together with the opulent Place Vendôme and elegant Palais Royal to the north, this quarter affords a glimpse into the extravagant life of the French rulers and the power and riches of the *ancien régime.*

PLACES TO SEE
Landmarks:
Terraces, alleys, slopes, stairways, and stone pools were carefully planned for the royal **Tuileries Gardens (27)** *(rue de Rivoli/Quai François Mitterrand, 1st, 01-40.20.90.43; hours: daily Apr–May 7AM–9PM, Jun–Aug 7AM–11PM, Sep–Mar 7:30AM–7:30PM)* situated along the Seine on the eastern border of Concorde. Statues by 19th- and

20th-century artists complete the architectural whole with magnificent vistas in every direction. The **Arc de Triomphe du Carrousel (28)**—built to celebrate Napoleon's 1805 victories—stands between the Tuileries and the Louvre. Stand beneath the arch for a fantastic view of Paris, stretching in a straight line from the Louvre through the Tuileries, past Concorde, along the Champs-Élysées, through the Arc de Triomphe, across to the Grand Arch at La Défense, just beyond Paris—an axis covering half the city. With nearly a third of a million works of art, the ★**LOUVRE MUSEUM (29)** *(rue de Rivoli, 1st, 01-40.20.53.17, www.louvre.fr; hours: M, Th, Sa–Su 9AM–6PM, W, F 9AM–9:45PM)* boasts one of the greatest art collections in the world. Formerly a medieval fortress and Renaissance royal palace, the Louvre became a museum after the Revolution. Its treasures include masterpieces of Egyptian, Etruscan, Greek, Roman, and Asian art, as well as more modern European works. Some of the most famous pieces are Leonardo da Vinci's *Mona Lisa*, the Greek *Winged Victory of Samothrace, Venus de Milo*, and the Assyrian *Winged Bull with Human Head*. A modern counterpoint to the museum's historic architectural splendor, I. M. Pei's striking 1989 glass **Louvre Pyramid (30)** *(courtyard)*, serves as the museum's main entrance. The surrounding reflecting pools create a dizzying mirror image of the glass and steel structure while small pyramids echo the larger one's effect. The

riverfront views are spectacular. Bordering the Tuileries and the Louvre to the north, **rue de Rivoli**, with its long row of arches, is home to expensive hotels, boutiques, and bookshops.

From rue de Rivoli, take rue de Castiglione and you'll arrive at one of Paris's most majestic squares, **Place Vendôme (31)** *(connecting to the Opéra via rue de la Paix)*. Built by Versailles architect Mansart, the octagonal square is an elegant example of harmonious, graceful 17th-century architecture. Many of the mansions were homes of bankers; one of them, No. 15, is now the **Hôtel Ritz (86)** *(see also page 59)*, where Coco Chanel lived, not far from her *salon de couture*. No. 12 was the house in which Chopin died in 1849. Today, under the arches encircling the square at ground level, **Place Vendôme (31)** is home to the haute jewelers of the world.

Just north of the Louvre is **Palais-Royal (32)** *(pl. du Palais-Royal, 1st, 01-47.03.92.16, palais-royal.monuments-nationaux.fr; hours: gardens daily Apr–May 7AM–10:15PM, Jun–Aug 7AM–11PM, Sep 7AM–9:30PM, Oct–Mar 7AM–8:30PM)*, once Cardinal Richelieu's palace, then the childhood home of Louis XIV, and later the scene of elaborate and lavish gatherings as well as gambling and indulgent, rowdy celebrations. Today its arched courtyard bustles with boutiques and restaurants. Not to be missed are the stunning early 19th-century shopping arcades (*passages* or *galeries*), with their high vaulted roofs of glass and iron. From the far (north) end of Palais-Royal, take rue Vivienne then turn right onto rue des Petits Champs.

To the left you'll find **Galerie Vivienne (33)** (*entrances at: 6 rue Vivienne, 4 rue des Petits-Champs, 5 rue de la Banque, 2nd, www.galerie-vivienne.com*) and **Galerie Colbert (34)** (*2 rue Vivienne, 2nd*)—wander into any *galerie*, but be sure to check out these two. Rue des Petits Champs turns into La Feuillade before reaching the elegant fashion mecca, **Place des Victoires (35)** (*rue la Feuillade, 1st/2nd*), built around a statue of Louis XIV.

Arts & Entertainment:

Museums abound: the **Louvre (29)** (*see also page 50*) for arts and antiquities, the **Jeu de Paume (36)** (*Jardin des Tuileries, pl. de la Concorde, 8th, 01-47.03.12.50, www. jeudepaume.org; hours: Tu 11AM–9PM, W–Su 11AM–7PM*) for contemporary art, the **Orangerie (37)** (*Jardin des Tuileries, pl. de la Concorde, 1st, 01-44.77.80.07, www.musee-orangerie.fr; hours: W–M 9AM–6PM*) for great Impressionist works, and the **Museum of Decorative Arts (38)** (*Palais de Louvre, 107 rue de Rivoli, 1st, 01-44.55.57.50, www.lesartsdecoratifs.fr; hours: Tu–Su 11AM–6PM, Th to 9PM*) for art and design and its Art Nouveau and Art Deco collections. Near the Palais-Royal entrance, France's finest classical theater is staged at the **Comédie Française (39)** (*2 rue de Richelieu, 1st, 08-25.10.16.80, from U.S. 011-33-1-44.58.15.15, www.comedie-francaise.fr; box office hours: daily 11AM–6PM; box office phone hours: M–Sa 11AM–6PM*). The **National Library-Richelieu Branch (40)** (*58 rue de Richelieu, 2nd, 01-53.79.59.59, www.bnf.fr; exhibition hours: Tu–Sa 10AM–7PM, Su 12PM–7PM*), north of Palais-Royal, became an exhibition space once its books were moved to the Mitterand branch. For a change of pace, **Legrand Filles et Fils (41)** *(1 rue de la Banque, 2nd, 01-42.60.07.12, www.caves-legrand.com; hours: M 11AM–7PM, Tu–F 10AM–7:30PM, Sa 10AM–7PM)* offers wine courses focusing on a region or producer.

PLACES TO EAT & DRINK
Where to Eat:

The area bordered by Tuileries, Concorde, Place Vendôme, and Palais-Royal is replete with cozy restaurants. Though Place Vendôme is one of the priciest spots in town, the nearby **L'Ardoise (42)** (€€) *(28 rue du Mont-Thabor, 1st, 01-42.96.28.18, www.lardoise-paris.com; hours: Tu–Sa 12PM–2:30PM, 6:30PM–11PM, Su 6:30PM–11PM)* is reasonably priced for good New Bistro fare. A few doors down, fashionistas feast on great burgers at lunch and tapas for dinner at **Ferdi (43)** (€€) *(32 rue du Mont-Thabor, 1st, 01-42.60.82.52; hours: Su–F 6:30PM–11:15PM, Sa 1:15PM–4:30PM, 7:30PM–11:15PM)*; you might spot Penélope Cruz there. Two doors away, **Le Soufflé (44)** (€€) *(36 rue du Mont-Thabor, 1st, 01-42.60.27.19, www.lesouffle.fr; hours: M–Sa 12PM–4:30PM, 7PM–10PM, book ahead, closed 3 wks Aug)*, an American favorite, offers a large variety of sweet and savory soufflés. Two streets down, quantity is the key word at **Lescure (45)** (€€) *(7 rue de Mondovi, 1st, 01-42.60.18.91; hours: M–F 12PM–2PM, 7PM–10PM)*, where the tables are so close together you can rub shoulders with your neighbor.

At **L'Écume St-Honoré (46)** (€-€€) *(6 rue du Marché-St-Honoré, 1st, 01-42.61.93.87; hours: Tu–F 8:30AM–2PM, 4PM–7:30PM, F until 10PM, Sa 8:30AM–10PM)*, you'll feel like you're in Brittany eating fresh oysters at a seaside shack. Communal wooden tables make brunch a rustic affair at **Le Pain Quotidien (47)** (€) *(18 pl. du Marché-St-Honoré, 1st, 01-42.96.31.70, www.lepainquotidien.com; hours: daily 8AM–10PM)*. Splurge at **Le Carré des Feuillants (48)** (€€€€) *(14 rue de Castiglione, 1st, 01-42.86.82.82, www.carredesfeuillants.fr; hours: M–F 12PM–2PM, 7:30PM–10PM, Sa 7:30PM–10PM)*, where the haute cuisine is fantastic and the service is superb. At least once, try the decadent desserts and rich hot chocolate at the old-world tea salon **Angelina (49)** (€) *(226 rue de Rivoli, 1st, 01-42.60.82.00, www.angelina-paris.fr; hours: M–F 7:30AM–7PM, Sa–Su 8:30AM–7PM)*.

One goes to **Café Marly (50)** (€€) *(93 rue de Rivoli, 1st, 01-49.26.06.60, www.louvre.fr/en/le-cafe-marly; hours: daily 8AM–2AM)*, facing I. M. Pei's pyramid, for its amazing setting and to see and be seen. The famous **Le Grand Véfour (51)** (€€€€) *(17 rue de Beaujolais, 1st, 01-42.96.56.27, www.grand-vefour.com; hours: M–F lunch and dinner, closed during Aug & Dec 24-31)*, bordering the gardens of Palais-Royal, is one of the most beautiful restaurants of Paris. Mirrors reflect the Napoleonic splendor of elegant ceiling and wall paintings, sculpted cornices, and hanging light fixtures. It was frequented by Colette, Jean Cocteau, Victor Hugo, and Napoleon. To avoid paying an arm and a leg, try the prix-fixe lunch. For good value and a brasserie that seems like it hasn't changed in decades, **L'Épi d'Or (52)** (€–€€) *(25 rue Jean-Jacques Rousseau, 1st, 01-42.36.38.12, www.faget-benard.com/jojo/epidor; hours: open M–Sa 12PM–2:30PM, 7:30PM–10:30PM)* has

"French" stamped all over it; best to reserve for dinner and be on time.

In the lavish Galerie Vivienne (33) *(see also page 52)* near Place des Victoires (35) *(see also page 52)*, an indoor terrace with glass arcade gives warmth to the upscale tea salon **A Priori Thé (53)** (€€) *(35-37 Galerie Vivienne, 2nd, 01-42.97.48.75, apriorithe.com; hours: M–F 9AM–6PM, Sa 9AM–6:30PM, Su brunch 12PM–4PM, Su tea 4PM–6:30PM)*; it also serves weekend brunch. On the other side of Place des Victoires (35), the trendy crowd flocks to the famous Parisian bistro **Chez Georges (54)** (€€€€) *(1 rue du Mail, 2nd, 01-42.60.07.11; hours: M–F 12PM–2:30PM, 7PM–11PM, closed Aug)* for an authentic experience of classic French food. Further north, across from the Bourse (old stock market), **Café Moderne (55)** (€€) *(40 rue Notre-Dame-des-Victoires, 2nd, 01-53.40.84.10; hours: M–F 12PM–2:30PM, 7:30PM–10:30PM)*—stylish, chic, yet cozy—boasts an eclectic menu with international flavors. Nearby, the draw at **Aux Lyonnais (56)** (€€) *(32 rue St-Marc, 2nd, 01-42.96.65.04, www.alain-ducasse.com; hours: Tu–F 12PM–2PM, 7:30PM–10PM, Sa 7:30PM–10PM, closed late Jul–late Aug)*, besides vintage bistro décor, is its owner, Alain Ducasse; the prices are very reasonable for Lyonnais cooking from this celebrated chef.

Bars & Nightlife:
Bar Vendôme (57) *(Hôtel Ritz, 15 pl. Vendôme, 1st, 01-43.16.30.30, www.ritzparis.com; hours: daily 10:30AM–2AM)*, coddled in velvet and mahogany, is a chic but intimate café-bar. A glass of champagne, a cup of tea,

and the melodic strains of the live piano exude both charm and luxury. The patio is a lovely spot for breakfast or a light lunch. **Le Café des Initiés (58)** *(3 pl. des Deux-Ecus, 1st, 01-42.33.78.29, www.lecafedesinities. com; hours: M–F 7:30AM–2AM, Sa–Su 9AM–2AM)* is a trendy *apéritif* hangout with friendly staff. For more elegance and a slightly colonial air, try **Le Fumoir (59)** *(6 rue de l'Amiral-de-Coligny, 1st, 01-42.92.00.24, www.lefumoir.com; hours: daily 11AM–2AM)*.

WHERE TO SHOP

Anne Sémonin (60) *(Place des Victoires, 2 rue des Petits Champs, 2nd, 01-42.60.94.66, www.annesemonin.com)* day spa and hair salon takes a holistic approach to beauty treatments. Walk through the arches of the rue de Rivoli, where boutiques and bookstores will catch your eye, including WH Smith (61) *(248 rue de Rivoli, 1st, 01-44.77.88.99, www.whsmith.fr; hours: M–Sa 9AM–7PM, Su 12:30PM–7PM)*, the renowned English bookseller. Across the rue de Rivoli from the Louvre, the Louvre des Antiquaires (62) *(2 pl. du Palais-Royal, 1st, 01-42.97.27.27, www.louvre-antiquaires.com; Tu–Su 11AM–7PM, closed Su in Jul–Aug)* houses 250 reputable dealers of high-quality antiques.

Fine jewels are the theme at **Place Vendôme (31)** *(see also page 51)*, where the great names of jewelry design sparkle with their gems: among them, Mauboussin (63) *(20 pl. Vendôme, 1st, 01-44.55.10.00, www.mauboussin.com; hours: M–Sa 10:30AM–7PM)*, Van Cleef & Arpels (64) *(22 pl. Vendôme, 1st, 01-55.04.11.12, www.vancleef-arpels.com; hours: M–F 10:30AM–7PM, Sa 11AM–7PM)*,

Boucheron (65) *(26 pl. Vendôme, 1st, 01-42.61.58.16, www.boucheron.com; hours: M–Sa 10:30AM–7PM)*, and Chanel (66) *(18 pl. Vendôme, 1st, 01-40.98.55.55, www.chanel.com; hours: M–Sa 10:30AM–6:30PM)*. For gems of another sort, take a whiff of jewelry designer Joel Rosenthal's exclusive perfumes at JAR (67) *(14 rue de Castiglione, 1st, 01-40.20.47.20)*. At the same address, sexy stilettos by Rodolphe Ménudier (68) *(5 & 14 rue de Castiglione, 1st, 06-07.02.81.91, 01-53.45.81.30, www.rodolphemenudier.com)* are sure to turn heads. For classic men's shirts and pajamas, Charvet (69) *(28 pl. Vendôme, 1st, 01-42.60.30.70, www.charvet.com)* has been shirtmaker to royalty and bourgeoisie since 1838.

Rue St-Honoré, just south of Place Vendôme (31) *(see also page 51)*, is one of the most famous shopping streets of Paris. To the west it's called rue du Faubourg-St-Honoré. As you walk eastward the shops go from extremely expensive couturiers to more moderate designer boutiques to the humbler shops of Les Halles. A few blocks east of Place Vendôme is an original Paris concept store, Colette (70) *(213 rue St-Honoré, 1st, 01-55.35.33.90, www.colette.fr; hours: M–Sa 11AM–7PM)*, a design emporium of clothing, art objects, and electronics, with a photo gallery, bookshop, and exhibition space. Jacques Le Corre-Destination 27 (71) *(191 rue St-Honoré, 1st, 01-42.60.39.27, www.jacqueslecorre.com)* designs stylish but practical hats, bags, and shoes.

In the Palais-Royal courtyard be sure to visit Italian costume jewelry designer Donatella Pellini's shop Pellini France (72) *(20 gal. de Montpensier, Jardins du Palais-Royal,*

1st, 01-42.96.18.68); her whimsical, elegant designs use stones and resins in cascades of colors and intriguing shapes. The destination for vintage haute couture is Didier Ludot (73) (20-24 gal. de Montpensier, Jardins du Palais-Royal, 1st, 01-42.96.06.56, www.didierludot.fr). Alongside the Palais-Royal, Martin Margiela (74) (25 bis, rue de Montpensier, 1st, 01-40.15.07.55, www.maison martinmargiela.com; hours: M–Sa 11AM–7PM), protégé of Jean Paul Gaultier, has opened his own boutique of inventive clothing and accessories. Perrin Paris 1893 (75) (35 rue des Petits Champs, 1st, 01-42.97.40.26, www.perrin paris.com; hours: M–F 11AM–6PM) specializes in chic handbags, gloves, and sunglasses. At Galerie Vivienne (33) (www.galerie-vivienne.com) you'll find stylish boutiques, such as Jean Paul Gaultier (76) (No. 6, Galerie Vivienne, 2nd, 01-42.86.05.05, www.jeanpaulgaultier.com). Populus Alba (77) (42 Galerie Vivienne, 2nd, 01-49.26.05.40, call for appt) showcases furniture designs, sculpture, and drawings by Christian Astuguevieille. For the little black beret, little black suit, little black cardigan, head to Claudie Pierlot (78) (1 rue du 29 Juillet, 1st, 01-42.60.01.19, www.claudiepierlot.com; hours: M–Sa 10:30AM–8PM). Galerie Véro-Dodat (79) (19 rue du Bouloi/Jean-Jacques Rousseau, 1st, 01-44.71.02.48) is another passage of antiquaries, vintage shops, and furniture designers.

Place des Victoires (35) (see also page 52) is the locus of major fashion boutiques, including Kenzo (80) (3 pl. des Victoires, 1st, 01-40.39.72.03, www.kenzo.com). You'll find apparel and accessory wonders at Lucien Pellat-Finet (81) (231 rue St-Honoré, 1st, 01-42.22.22.77, www.

lucienpellat-finet.com). Sandrine Philippe (82) *(6 rue Hérold, 1st, 01-40.26.21.78, www.sandrinephilippe.com)* designs sophisticated, romantic fashions with a way of making you feel like you're part of a story behind her clothes. The signature cuts and finishes of Yohji Yamamoto (83) *(4 rue Cambon, 1st, 01-40.20.00.71, www.yohji yamamoto.co.jp),* are inspired by the kimono.

WHERE TO STAY

Clean and comfortable, Hôtel Vivienne (84) (€) *(40 rue Vivienne, 2nd, 01-42.33.13.26, www.hotel-vivienne.com)* is a good budget hotel. The best rooms at Hôtel Brighton (85) (€€-€€€) *(218 rue de Rivoli, 1st, 01-47.03.61.61, www.paris-hotel-brighton.com, www.esprit-de-france.com)* have great views. Overlooking the Tuileries Gardens, the very expensive Hôtel Meurice (86) (€€€€) *(228 rue de Rivoli, 1st, 01-44.58.10.10, www.lemeurice.com)* boasts a discerning clientele and its spa is divine. Pure, unabashed luxury reigns at the Hôtel Ritz (87) (€€€€) *(15 pl. Vendôme, 1st, 01-43.16.30.30, www.ritzparis.com; has been closed for renovations; check Web site for updates).* If you don't like flamboyance, Hôtel Costes (88) (€€€€) *(239 rue St-Honoré, 1st, 01-42.44.50.00, www.hotelcostes.com)* isn't for you. More intimate, with painted beams and picturesque furnishings, is Le Relais St-Honoré (89) (€€-€€€) *(308 rue St-Honoré, 1st, 01-42.96.06.06, www.relaissainthonore. com)*—you might think you've been transported to a charming country manor. And within walking distance from Palais-Royal, Hôtel Thérèse (90) (€€-€€€) *(5-7 rue Thérèse, 1st, 01-42.96.10.01, www.hoteltherese.com)* offers subdued luxury.

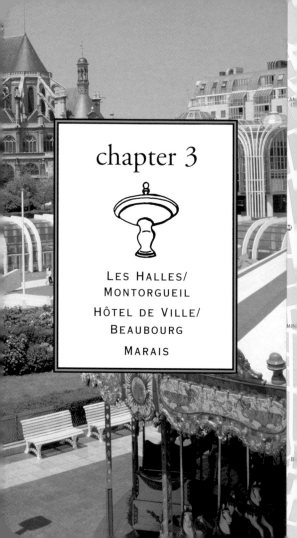

chapter 3

LES HALLES/
MONTORGUEIL
HÔTEL DE VILLE/
BEAUBOURG
MARAIS

LES HALLES/MONTORGUEIL
HÔTEL DE VILLE/BEAUBOURG
MARAIS

Places to See:

1. Forum des Halles
2. Halles Garden
3. Fontaine des Innocents
4. Rue Montorgueil
5. St-Eustache
6. Bourse de Commerce
7. Tour Jean Sans Peur
8. Théâtre du Châtelet
49. Place du Châtelet
50. Théâtre de la Ville
51. Tour St-Jacques
52. Hôtel de Ville
53. St. Gervais-St. Protais
54. Rue des Barres
55. St-Merri
56. CENTRE GEORGES
    POMPIDOU ★
57. Fontaine de Stravinsky
58. Rue Quincampoix
59. Auberge Nicolas Flamel
60. IRCAM
61. Musée de la Poupée
62. Musée d'Art et d'Histoire
    du Judaïsme
63. L'Atelier de Fred
64. Musée des Arts et Métiers
77. Hôtel de Sens

78. Shoah Memorial
79. Hôtel de Sully
80. Place des Vosges
81. Victor Hugo House
82. Musée Carnavalet
83. Musée Cognacq-Jay
84. Picasso Museum
85. Hôtel de Rohan
86. Hôtel de Soubise
87. Cloître des Billettes
88. Rue Vieille-du-Temple
89. Rue Ste-Croix-de-la-
    Bretonnerie
90. Museum of Magic
91. Maison Européenne de la
    Photographie
92. La Galerie d'Architecture

Places to Eat & Drink:

9. Au Pied de Cochon
10. Au Petit Creux
11. Chez Denise—La Tour de
    Montlhéry
12. Le Père Fouettard
13. Au Chien qui Fume
14. Le Louchebem
15. L' Hédoniste
16. Yam'Tcha

★ *Top Pick*

LES HALLES/MONTORGUEIL

④ to Les Halles; ① ④ ⑦ ⑪ ⑭ to Châtelet;
⑦ to Pont Neuf; ① to Louvre-Rivoli;
④ to Étienne Marcel; ③ to Sentier;
③④ to Réaumur-Sébastopol;
④⑧⑨ to Strasbourg-St-Denis

• SNAPSHOT •

Les Halles was once the farmers' market of Paris, sheltered beneath beautiful glass and cast-iron pavilions. When Émile Zola dubbed it "the belly of Paris," he was referring to the food market, but the description applied equally to the unsavory and "alternate" characters who inhabited the area. The pavilions were demolished in 1969 and were later replaced by the Forum des Halles, an underground mall and transportation hub. A mixed mass of humanity still crowds the streets, and rue St-Denis has long been a red-light district, but there are plenty of remarkable spots in Les Halles. More picturesque, however, is the hip Montorgueil area, directly north of the Forum. The small streets around rue Tiquetonne and rue Étienne Marcel turn up funky

corners and trendy finds. All-night bistros thrive in Les Halles, while Montorgueil is crammed with romantic cafés as well as food and wine merchants slightly reminiscent of the old Halles.

PLACES TO SEE
Landmarks:

The **Forum des Halles (1)** *(rues Rambuteau/Pierre Lescot/Berger, 1st)* is a three-level mall with shops, cinemas, and a pool. Despite its open central courtyard, it's rather gloomy. The surrounding landscape, the **Halles Garden (2)** *(west of Forum des Halles, 1st)*, is as devoid of charm as the Forum. Architecture and city planning buffs are challenged by this bad 1970s attempt at urban renewal. Kitty-cornered (SE) from the Forum is the **Fontaine des Innocents (3)** *(rue Berger/rue Pierre Lescot, 1st)*, a Renaissance fountain erected on the site of the Innocents Cemetery, from which vast numbers of corpses were moved in 1785 to the Catacombs *(see Chapter 6, page 162)*. North of Les Halles, you'll discover a more soulful area. Stroll along the narrow **rue Montorgueil (4)** *(1st)* and take in the flavors of the fruit and vegetable vendors, the wine and cheese merchants, and the ubiquitous cafés.

Here you'll also find one of Paris's most magnificent churches, **St-Eustache (5)** *(rue du Jour, 1st, 01.42. 36.31.05, www.st-eustache.org; hours: M–F 9:30AM– 7PM, Sa 10AM–7PM, Su 9AM–7PM)*, north of the **Halles Garden (2)** *(see also above)*. Modeled on Notre-Dame, with its flying buttresses, its plan is Gothic, but the decoration is sumptuously Renaissance. Historic figures are affiliated with this church, where Cardinal Richelieu and the Marquise de Pompadour (Louis XV's official mistress) were baptized. Another interesting building is nearby: at the east end of the **Halles Garden (2)**, the **Bourse de Commerce (6)** *(2 rue de Viarmes, 1st,*

01-42.33.06.67, www.sgbcp.fr; hours: by appt M–F 9AM–6PM) provides group tours of this commodities market.

The **Tour Jean Sans Peur (7)** *(20 rue Étienne Marcel, 2nd, 01-40.26.20.28, www.tourjeansanspeur.com; hours: Apr–Nov W–Su 1:30PM–6PM, Nov–Mar W, Sa–Su 1:30PM–6PM)* was the Duke of Burgundy's attempt to protect himself from reprisals after he assassinated his rival, the Duke of Orleans, which was believed to have ignited the Hundred Years' War. Burgundian symbols— oak, hawthorn, and hops—are carved into the turret. Rues Montorgueil, Tiquetonne, and Étienne Marcel are fun, funky places to explore around the Forum and are a bit more appealing to the eyes.

Arts & Entertainment:

The free recitals at **St-Eustache (5)** *(Su 5:30PM), (see also page 65)* feature its 8,000-pipe organ. **Théâtre du Châtelet (8)** *(1 pl. du Châtelet, 1st, west side of the square, 01-40.28.28.40, www.chatelet-theatre.com)* is one of Paris's main venues for classical music, opera, and dance; its annual *Bleu sur Scène* blues festival brings major artists, like Herbie Hancock and Ornette Coleman.

PLACES TO EAT & DRINK
Where to Eat:

Though fast-food joints glut Les Halles, you can eat well nearby. A stone's throw from the **Bourse de Commerce (6)** *(see also page 65)* is a brasserie once frequented by market workers: **Au Pied de Cochon (9)** **(€€-€€€)** *(6 rue Coquillière, 1st, 01-40.13.77.00, www.pieddecochon.com; hours: open 24/7)* serves such classics as onion soup and oysters, but its specialty is grilled pig's feet in béarnaise sauce. Several eateries south of Halles offer good deals. Locals and budget-minded travelers enjoy the home-made lunch selections at friendly **Au Petit Creux (10)** **(€)** *(8 rue Roule, 1st, 01-42.36.80.46; hours: M–Sa noon–5PM)*. Fun, friendly, and open all night, **Chez Denise—La Tour de Montlhéry (11)** **(€€-€€€)** *(5 rue des Prouvaires, 1st, 01-42.36.21.82; hours: M–F 12PM–3PM, 7:30PM–5AM)* serves excellent classics and is frequented by artists, writers, and business "suits" alike. Inexpensive and relaxing, **Le Père Fouettard (12)** **(€)** *(9 rue Pierre Lescot, 1st, 01-42.33.74.17, www.brasserie-flottes.fr/au-pere-fouettard; hours: daily 7:30AM–2AM)* has a year-round terrace. **Au Chien qui Fume (13)** **(€€)** *(33 rue du Pont-Neuf, 1st, 01-42.36.07.42, www.auchienquifume.com; hours: daily 12PM–2AM)* serves brasserie favorites, including braised rabbit; the décor's motif is dogs dressed as people—the place is, after all, "The Smoking Dog." **Le Louchebem (14)** **(€-€€)** *(31 rue Berger, 1st, 01-42.33.12.99, www.le-louchebem.fr; hours: M–Sa open to 11:30PM)* is a steak lover's haven. For modern French cuisine with a creative flair, natural wines, and reasonable prices, try **L'Hédoniste (15)** **(€-€€)** *(14 rue Léopold Bellan, 2nd, 01-40.26.87.33,* *www.lhedoniste.com;* hours: *Tu–Th 12:30PM–2PM, 8PM–10:15PM, F 12:30PM–2PM, 8PM–11PM, Sa 8PM–11PM).* At **Yam'Tcha (16)** (€€–€€€) *(4 rue Sauval, 1st, 01-40.26.08.07, www.yamtcha.com; hours: Tu 7PM–10:30PM, W–Sa 10AM–3:30PM, 7PM–10:30PM)* rising culinary star Adeline Grattard gives French touches to delicate, creative Chinese cuisine.

In the Montorgueil area, **La Potée des Halles (17)** (€–€€) *(3 rue Étienne Marcel, 1st, 01-45.08.50.11; hours: M, W–F 12PM–2:30PM, 7PM–11:30PM, Tu 12PM–2:30PM, Sa–Su 7PM–11:30PM, closed Aug)* is steamy with beans, cabbage, pork, and veal. Classified a national monument, its hand-painted tiled walls depict beer and coffee goddesses. The original chairs bear the names of Halles worker regulars; some of them still are, at 70 or 80. Another working-class haunt, **Le Christ Inn's Bistrot (18)** (€) *(15 rue Montmartre, 1st, 01-42.36.07.56; hours: Tu–Sa 12PM–10:30PM)* serves hearty portions to a mostly French clientele. In the lively food market street, rue Montorgueil (4) *(see also page 65),* **Foody's Brunch Café (19)** (€) *(26 rue Montorgueil, 1st, 01-40.13.02.53; hours: M–Sa 11:30AM–5PM, closed first 3 wks Aug)* is a self-service vegetarian restaurant with soups, salads, fresh juice, and bakery goods at great prices. Select your side dishes to go with your main course at fun and friendly **Le Loup Blanc (20)** (€–€€) *(42 rue Tiquetonne, 2nd, 01-40.13.08.35; www.loup-blanc.com; hours: daily 7:30PM–12AM).* **La Crêpe Dentelle (21)** (€) *(8 rue Léopold Bellan, 2nd, 01-40.41.04.23; hours: M–F 11:30AM–3:30PM, 7:30PM–*

11PM, Sa 7:30PM–11PM) is a family-run *crêperie* serving an array of delicious crêpes and indulgent desserts. The oldest *pâtisserie* in Paris, classified as a historical monument, **Stohrer (22)** (€) *(51 rue Montorgueil, 2nd, 01-42.33.38.20, www.stohrer.fr; hours: daily 7:30AM–8:30PM)* was opened in 1730 by Marie Antoinette's personal baker. Now we know why she said, "Let them eat cake!" Around the corner, at classic **Aux Crus de Bourgogne (23)** (€-€€) *(3 rue Bachaumont, 2nd, 01-42.33.48.24, www.auxcrusdebourgogne.com; hours: M–F 12PM–2:30PM, 7:45PM–10:30PM)*, nostalgia is served up with the house specialty, fresh lobster.

Bars & Nightlife:

Hot spot **Kong (24)** *(1 rue du Pont-Neuf, 1st, 01-40.39.09.00, www.kong.fr; hours: happy hour daily 6PM–8PM, music bar daily 10:30PM–2AM, restaurant daily 10:30AM–2AM)* was designed by Philippe Starck and featured on *Sex and the City*—the too-cool staff is part of the heavy-on-style, light-on-substance ambience. Dance the night away, from swing to rock 'n' roll, at **NY Club Paris (25)** *(130 rue de Rivoli, 1st, 01-42.33.84.30, www.nyclubparis.com; hours: daily 11PM–6AM)*, on the footprint of famous jazz clubs that have changed over the years. **Rue des Lombards** in Les Halles is known for live jazz. Among its notable clubs are **Au Duc des Lombards (26)** *(42 rue des Lombards, 1st, 01-42.33.22.88, www.ducdeslombards.com; hours: M–Sa, call for hours)* and **Baiser Salé (27)** *(58 rue des Lombards, 1st, 01-42.33.37.71, www.lebaisersale.com; call for hours)*.

At **Le Sunset/Le Sunside (28)** *(60 rue des Lombards, 1st, 01-40.26.46.60, www.sunset-sunside.com; call for hours)*, artists from both sides of the Atlantic play (electric in the former; acoustic, the latter). Lively **Bistrot d'Eustache (29)** **(€€-€€€)** *(37 rue Berger, 1st, 01-40.26.23.20; call for hours)*, a charming throwback to the jazz age of the 1930s and 1940s, serves traditional French food; the jazz is live, with Gypsy guitar jazz on Thursday nights. North of the area, no-frills jazz mainstay **New Morning (30)** *(7 rue Petites-Ecuries, 10th, north of our map border, check Web site for location, 01-45.23.51.41, www.newmorning.com; hours: opens nightly at 8PM)* attracts true jazz fanatics and some of the world's most renowned musical artists. Take a wine-tasting lunch, dinner, or day trip with **Ô Chateau (31)** *(68 rue Jean-Jacques Rousseau, 1st, 01-44.73.97.80, www.o-chateau.com)*. Its relaxed wine bar *(hours: M–Sa 4PM–12AM)* offers a wine of the day for 5€ a glass. Sample delights from its kitchen **(€€-€€€)**, run by Cordon Bleu graduates. Visit its Web site for all the options and prices and book ahead.

WHERE TO SHOP

La Grande Boutique de l'Artisan Parfumeur (32) *(2 rue l'Amiral Coligny, 1st, 01-44.88.27.50, www.artisanparfumeur.com)* is the flagship store of the grand perfume specialist. The place also offers workshops on the art and history of perfumery.

A baker's delight, G. Detou (33) *(58 rue Tiquetonne, 2nd, 01-42.33.96.43, 01-42.36.54.67, gdetou.com; hours: M–Sa 8:30AM–6:30PM)* means "a bit of everything," and you'll find just that on its shelves: chocolates, nuts, sugars, dragees, spices, plus teas, mustards, and much, much more. You'll find all manner of kitchen utensils and tableware at E. Dehillerin (34) *(18 rue Coquillière, 1st, 01-42.36.53.13, www.e-dehillerin.fr; hours: M 9AM–12:30PM, 2PM–6PM, Tu–Sa 9AM–6PM)*, A. Simon (35) *(48 rue Montmartre, 2nd, 01-42.33.71.65)*, and Mora (36) *(13 rue Montmartre, 1st, 01-45.08.19.24, www.mora.fr; hours: M–F 9AM–6:15PM, Sa 10AM–1PM, 1:45PM–6:30PM)*. For beads, ribbon, buttons, and yarn, visit La Droguerie (37) *(9-11 rue du Jour, 1st, 01-45.08.93.27, www.ladroguerie.com; hours: M 2PM–6:45PM, Tu–Sa 10:30AM–6:45PM)*. Rue du Jour has spawned a small Agnès b (38) *(2, 3, 4, 6 rue du Jour, 1st, women 01-45.08.56.56, men 01-42.33.04.13, travel 01-40.13.91.27, children 01-40.39.96.88, europe.agnesb.com/fr)* empire, where black is the staple wardrobe color and bright patterns are mixed in for fun.

Buy last season's fashions at outlet prices at Et Vous Stock (39) (*17 rue Turbigo, 2nd, 01-40.13.04.12*). When the walking gets to you, enter the medieval stone walls of Spa Nuxe (40) (*32 rue Montorgueil, 1st, 01-42.36.65.65, www.nuxe.com*) for an exotic serene experience of their treatments, or just pick up a few beauty products. Conversely, try the hammam (Turkish bath) at Aux Bains Montorgueil (41) (*55 rue Montorgueil, 2nd, 01-44.88.01.78; hours: Tu–Su 10AM–9PM, appt. only*) for a steam bath, an exfoliation, and a massage. If sewing and crafts are your passion, don't miss Declercq Passementiers (42) (*15 rue Étienne Marcel, 1st, 01-44.76.90.70, www.declercq passementiers.fr*) for fantastic trimmings and tassels. Walk along the trendy **rue Étienne Marcel**, lined with hip names in fashion—Yohji Yamamoto, Joseph, and Diesel, among others. In the Montorgueil quarter, **rue Tiquetonne** is a trendsetter. It's full of workshops, restaurants, and boutiques, including Kiliwatch (43) (*64 rue Tiquetonne, 2nd, 01-42.21.17.37, www.espacekiliwatch. fr; hours: M 2PM–7:15PM, Tu–Sa 11AM–7:45PM*), a designer and secondhand clothing store. Increasingly popular, it sells used fashions by the kilo. Gourmet cookbooks, old and new, abound at Librairie Gourmande (44) (*92-96 rue Montmartre, 2nd, 01-43.54.37.27, www.librairiegourmande.fr; hours: M–Sa 11AM–7PM*): they include French, American, and English editions. Between rue St-Denis and rue Dussoubs, is the Passage du Grand Cerf (45) (*145 rue St-Denis/8 rue Dussoubs, 2nd, www.passagedugrandcerf.com; hours:*

M–Sa 8:30AM–8PM), with its Belle Époque ironwork and funky, fashionable purveyors of clothing, accessories, lighting, and art objects; prominent shops include **As'Art** *(No. 3)*, for unique African and ethnic gifts, **MX Sylvie Branellec** *(No. 6)*, with jewelry focused on pearls, and **PM CO Style** *(No. 5)*, for a variety of fascinating design objects from the far corners of Earth. Saïki (46) *(32 rue Etienne Marcel, 2nd, 01-42.33.74.30, www.saiki.fr)* is a tiny boutique stocking wonderful handmade jewelry.

WHERE TO STAY

Les Halles isn't the best place to stay, but the Montorgueil area affords some bargains. Ambience is missing at the **Tiquetonne Hotel (47)** (€) *(6 rue Tiquetonne, 2nd, 01-42.36.94.58, hoteltiquetonne.fr)*, but it's cheap, clean, and very, very basic (with chenille bedspreads). **Hôtel du Cygne (48)** (€) *(3 rue du Cygne, 1st, 01-42.60.14.16, www.hotelducygne.fr)* is reliable, appealing, and livable, with rooms decorated in Laura Ashley style.

HÔTEL DE VILLE/BEAUBOURG

① ④ ⑦ ⑪ ⑭ *to Châtelet;*
① ⑪ *to Hôtel de Ville;* ⑪ *to Rambuteau;*
③ ⑪ *to Arts et Métiers;*
③ ④ *to Réaumur-Sébastopol;*
④ ⑧ ⑨ *to Strasbourg-St-Denis*

• SNAPSHOT •

Dominated by the Hôtel de Ville (town hall) and the Centre Georges Pompidou (colloquially referred to as "Beaubourg"), this district is jam-packed with interesting landmarks, museums, bars, and shops. Two aesthetics coexist: the ornate marble—replete with turrets and statues—of the Hôtel de Ville corresponds to the pomp and circumstance of its stature; a few streets away the "inside-out" structure of Beaubourg—with color-coded pipes, scaffolding, and ducts—puts the functional works of the building on public display. The district is exciting and vibrant, attracting a crowd eager for street spectacles —and there are plenty of those in the Hôtel de Ville/ Beaubourg quarter.

PLACES TO SEE
Landmarks:

Start at **Place du Châtelet (49)** *(at bd. De Sébastopol, 4th)*. Once a fortress defending the city from the north, it is now a major Métro hub. Above ground, in the center of the square, is a fountain—yet another monument to Napoleon's victories. On either side of

Place du Châtelet (49) are the twin theaters Théâtre du Châtelet (8) *(west side; see page 66)* and Théâtre de la Ville (50) *(east side; 2 pl. du Châtelet, 4th, 01-42.74.22.77, www.theatredelaville-paris.com)*. In the northeast corner, the Tour St-Jacques (51) *(Sq. de la Tour St-Jacques, 4th)* seems to oversee the area. The Flamboyant Gothic tower is what is left standing of a church that served as the meeting point for pilgrims before they ventured out on their travels. The tower was a favorite of the Surrealists, perhaps because of the plethora of gargoyles or because of their incongruity with the figure at the base of the tower, a statue of Blaise Pascal, who conducted barometrical experiments at the site in the 17th century.

As you walk along the *quai* (embankment) of the Seine eastward, gaze along the river at the fabulous views. Across the Seine, you'll see the old Conciergerie prison *(see Chapter 5, page 125)*; further to the left, the cathedral of Notre-Dame *(see Chapter 5, page 126)*; and in the distance to the right, the Eiffel Tower *(see Chapter 1, page 24)*. Great photo ops! Continuing along the *quai*, you'll arrive at the Hôtel de Ville (52) *(pl. de l'Hôtel de Ville, 29 rue de Rivoli, 4th, 01-42.76.43.43, www.paris.fr; hours: M–Sa 10AM–7PM)*, which serves as town hall, city council premises, and official residence of the mayor of Paris. It is also the venue for receptions honoring foreign dignitaries. With its elaborate, sculpted exterior and the impressive interior adorned with chandeliers, statues, caryatids, and a majestic staircase, the Hôtel de Ville (52) exudes power, pomp, and ceremony. The square facing the building has had its share of power-filled days: it was once the main site for public executions.

East of the **Hôtel de Ville (52)** is the 6th-century church **St. Gervais-St. Protais (53)** *(pl. St-Gervais, 4th, 01.48.87.32.02, www. paris.catholique.fr; hours: daily 6AM–9PM)*, the façade of which is made up of three levels of columns—Doric, Ionic, and Corinthian. This beautiful church is famous for its religious music. Walk around the back, up the picturesque **rue des Barres (54)** *(rue François Miron/rue de l'Hotel de Ville, 4th)* where artists set up their easels and small cafés cover the terraced sidewalk with tables and chairs. A few streets northwest-ward is the 7th-century church of **St-Merri (55)** *(76 rue de la Verrerie, 4th, 01-42.71.93.93, www.saintmerri.org; hours: daily 12PM–7PM)*, decidedly Gothic.

Follow the rue St-Martin two streets north and you'll come to the **★CENTRE GEORGES POMPIDOU (56)**, or "Beaubourg" *(pl. Georges Pompidou/rue Beaubourg, 4th, 01-44.78.12.33, www.centrepompidou.fr; hours: W–M 11AM–9PM)*. Opened in 1977, it was an immediate success and has remained so; its inside-out structure makes it one of the most unique examples of modern architecture. The workings of the building—air ducts, water shafts, utility pipes, elevators, escalators, and structural steel struts—are all on the outside, color-coded to distinguish their functions, while the glass and steel walls give a sense of interior-exterior permeability. This leaves the entire interior space with the flexibility to adapt to the center's activities and needs. The museum boasts a collection of more than 50,000 works, covering painting, sculpture,

TOP PICK!

drawing, photography, architecture, design, cinema, video, and audio-visual archives in addition to a library, screening rooms, and performance and exhibition spaces.

Outside Beaubourg, on the large esplanade, pavement artists and street performers do their thing to crowds of willing onlookers. South of Beaubourg, the **Fontaine de Stravinsky (57)** *(pl. Igor Stravinsky, rue Brismiche, 4th)*, created by artists Niki de St-Phalle and Jean Tinguely, is an intermingling orchestra of delightfully colorful and fanciful creature sculptures, each contributing to the waterworks extravaganza. Along **rue Quincampoix (58)** *(rue des Lombards/rue Rambuteau, 4th)*, a bevy of galleries, cafés, and bars animate the cobblestone street and its restored 18th-century residences. A block past its northern end is the (probably) oldest house in Paris: **Auberge Nicolas Flamel (59)** *(51 rue de Montmorency, 3rd, 01-42.71.77.78, www.auberge-nicolas-flamel.fr, hours: M–Sa 12PM–2:30PM, 7PM–10:30PM)* is one of Paris's oldest homes (home closed to public) and restaurants **(€€€)**, dating to 1407.

Arts & Entertainment:

Théâtre de la Ville (50) *(see also page 76)* is a must-stop for modern dance fans, where many important choreographers, such as Maguy Marin and Jean-Claude Gallotta, have showcased their talents. The modern art exhibits, audio-visual screenings, and performance art at **Centre Georges Pompidou (56)** *(see also page 77)* are not to be missed. By the southern flank of Centre Pompidou, **IRCAM (60)** *(1 pl. Igor Stravinsky, 4th, 01-44.78.48.43, www.ircam.fr; call for show hours)*, dedicated to musical experimentation and research, offers contemporary music concerts; Pierre Boulez has been actively involved in IRCAM since its conception. A street north of Beaubourg, the **Musée de la Poupée (61)** *(impasse Berthaud, 3rd, 01-42.72.73.11, www.museedelapoupeeparis.com; hours: Tu–Sa 10AM–6PM)* exhibits dolls from around the world, has a doll hospital, and offers doll-making classes for adults and children. The **Musée d'Art et d'Histoire du Judaïsme (62)** *(Hôtel de St-Aignan, 71 rue du Temple, 3rd, 01-53.01.86.53, www.mahj.org; hours: M–F 11AM–6PM, Su 10AM–6PM)* is dedicated to French Jewish culture from the Middle Ages to the present. Take cooking classes (small groups) at **L'Atelier de Fred (63)** *(6 rue des Vertus, 3rd, 01-40.29.46.04, www.latelierdefred.com)* to impress your friends back home with an authentic, homemade Parisian meal. The **Musée des Arts et Métiers (64)** (Museum of Science and Industry) *(60 rue Réaumur, 3rd, 01-53.01.82.00, www.arts-et-metiers.net; hours: Tu–Su 10AM–6PM, Th 10AM–9:30PM)* hosts conferences ranging from cloud computing to how to anticipate natural disasters; among other inventive objects, the mechanical figures and prototype machines are amusing.

PLACES TO EAT & DRINK
Where to Eat:

Dine at the ancient home of a famed alchemist at **Auberge Nicolas Flamel (59) (€€€)** *(see also page 78)*. Fondue fans fancy **Pain, Vin, Fromages (65) (€)** *(3 rue de Geoffroy l'Angevin, 4th, 01-42.74.07.52, www.painvin fromage.com; hours: daily 7AM–11:30PM)*. The menu offers other choices, too. Wholesome breakfast, brunch, and lunch options with a vegetarian focus make **Bob's Kitchen (66) (€)** *(74 rue des Gravilliers, 3rd, 09-52.55.11.66, www.bobsjuicebar.com; hours: M–F 8AM–3PM, Sa–Su 10AM–4PM)* a favorite of visitors and Parisians. "Bob" also has a popular juice bar in the 10th arrondissement. Take in the sights, from the fashion-model wait staff to the Parisian rooftops and major gems of the city, at **Georges (67) (€€€)** *(Centre Pompidou, 19 rue Beaubourg, 4th, 01-44.78.47.99, www.maison thierrycostes.com; hours: W–M 12PM–3PM, 7:30PM–11PM)*, the ultra-chic café-restaurant on the terrace of Beaubourg; the food's good and the view is superlative. Best for drinks, light fare, and brunch, **Café Beaubourg (68) (€€)** *(100 rue St-Martin/43 rue St-Merri, 4th, 01-48.87.63.96, wwwmaisonthierrycostes.com; hours: M–Th 8AM–1AM, F 8AM–2AM, Sa 9AM–2AM, Su 9AM–1AM; for lunch & dinner book ahead)* offers its fashionable patrons a great place from which to people watch. For classic French dishes that are simple but surprising, **Le Hangar (69) (€€)** *(12 impasse Berthaud, 3rd, 01-42.74.55.44, cash only; hours: Tu–Sa 12PM–2:30PM, 7:30PM–11PM, closed Aug)*, a cozy bistro by the doll museum, is one of the best values in Paris. Around the corner is another great find:

good food and friendly staff are served up at **Le Petit Marcel (70) (€)** *(65 rue Rambuteau, 4th, 01-48.87.10.20; hours: daily 8AM–1AM)*. **Le 404 (71) (€€)** *(69 rue des Gravilliers, 3rd, 01-42.74.57.81, 404-resto.com; hours: M–F 12PM–2:30PM, 7:30PM–11:30PM, Sa–Su 12PM–4PM, 7:30PM–11:30PM)* is a fabulous Moroccan restaurant that's funky, sexy, and noisy; get down with the table-dancing crowd. Tiny but popular and friendly, **Le Potager du Marais (72) (€)** *(24 rue Rambuteau, 3rd, 01-57.40.98.57, www.lepotagerdumarais.fr; hours: daily 12PM–12AM)* has great vegetarian food.

Bars & Nightlife:

Andy Wahloo (73) *(69 rue Gravilliers, 3rd, 01-42.71.20.38, andywahloo-bar.com; hours: Tu–Sa 7PM–1:45AM)*, a North African bar next door to **Le 404 (71)** *(http://404-resto.com; see also above)*, has an industrial décor and amicable staff ready to serve beer, cocktails, and hookahs.

WHERE TO SHOP

Elegance is the byword at **Heaven (74)** *(16 rue du Pont Louis-Philippe, 4th, 01-42.77.38.89, www.heaven-paris.com; hours: Tu–Sa 11AM–7:30PM, Su 2PM–7:30PM)*, where a fashion designer and lighting creator have teamed up to showcase their works. Fun and whimsical gifts of all sorts fill **Fleux (75)** *(39 & 52 rue Ste Croix la Bretonnerie, 4th, 01-42.78.27.20, 01-42.77.73.85, www.fleux.com; hours: M–F 11AM–7:30PM, Sa 10:30AM–8PM, Su 2PM–7PM)*. The designers and artists showcased at **FR66 (76)** *(25 rue du Renard, 4th, 01-44.54.35.36; hours: M–Sa 10AM–7PM, closed 2–3 wks Aug)*, a shop that sometimes seems more like a gallery, create unique items for the home.

MARAIS

7 *to Pont Marie;* **1** *to St. Paul;*
8 *to Chemin Vert or St-Sébastien-Froissart*

• SNAPSHOT •

Likely the most fascinating quarter of Paris, the Marais is also one of the most beautiful. Its exquisite character comes partly from a successful combination of diverse cultures and styles. Old elegance is embodied in the 17th-century mansions, expertly restored in the 1960s. These coexist harmoniously with boutiques displaying contemporary art, fashion, and culture. At the same time, small artisans and shopkeepers have held their own against the tide of gentrification, as have the old Jewish quarter and other ethnic neighborhoods. The entry of a vibrant gay culture has brought with it renewal and its own fashion and culture. Galleries, original new designers, bookshops, boutiques, and exhibition spaces line streets such as rue Vieille-du-Temple, rue Debelleyme, rue Charlot, rue des Rosiers, and rue du Roi-de-Sicile. The café culture too is strong. The historical landmarks, superb architecture, and romantic narrow streets garnished with coach lamps and ironwork add to the magic of the scene.

PLACES TO SEE
Landmarks:

Just past the **Pont-Marie** and one street in from the river, **Hôtel de Sens (77)** *(1 rue du Figuier, 4th, 01-42.78.14.60; hours: Tu–F 1:30PM–8:30PM, Sa 10AM–8:30PM, closed 2 weeks in July)*, now home to the Forney fine arts library, is a rare medieval building built between 1475 and 1507, its turrets and arches evocative of a time when Bourbons, Guises, and Cardinal de Pellevé occupied the premises. Just westward, at the border of the Jewish quarter, the **Shoah Memorial (78)** *(17 rue Geoffroy-l'Asnier, 4th, 01-42.77.44.72 www.memorialdelashoah.org; hours: Su–W, F 10AM–6PM, Th 10AM–10PM)*, with its Memorial to the Unknown Jewish Martyr, is a memorial, study center, and museum dedicated to the Holocaust. **Rue des Rosiers**, a once colorful area, is fast being taken over by chain stores, and its old Jewish character is fading. The **Hôtel de Sully (79)** *(62 rue St-Antoine, 4th, 01-44.61.20.00; 01-42.78.49.32; hours: Tu–Su 10AM–7PM)*, a beautiful late-Renaissance mansion, houses the Center for National Monuments.

A step away is the heart of the Marais, the **Place des Vosges (80)** *(rue des Francs Bourgeois, 4th)*. Perhaps the most lovely and aesthetically pleasing square in the world, it's perfectly symmetrical: 36 houses, equally placed on four sides, stand gracefully over rows of arcades. Red brick and stone façades with slate blue roofs and dormer windows lend a

simple yet regal elegance to the large square, where jousts, tournaments, and historic events took place. Literati, such as Madame de Sévigné, held salons here. The **Victor Hugo House (81)** *(6 pl. des Vosges, 4th, 01-42.72.10.16, www.musee-hugo.paris.fr; hours: Tu–Su 10AM–6PM)* is where the writer lived and where *Les Misérables* was created. Stroll under the arcades to find a variety of shops, galleries, and cafés—it's where Inspector Maigret of the Simenon detective novels likes to sip a *café-au-lait*.

Explore the many stunning small streets in the area as you make your way northward toward the **Musée Carnavalet (82)** *(23 rue de Sévigné, 3rd, 01-44.59.58.58, www.carnavalet.paris.fr; hours: Tu–Sa 10AM–6PM)*, a mansion dedicated to the history of Paris *(see also page 86)*. One street westward, you have the opportunity to enter an old Marais home: the **Musée Cognacq-Jay (83)** *(Hôtel de Donon, 8 rue Elzévir, 3rd, 01-40.27.07.21, www.cognacq-jay.paris.fr; hours: Tu–Su 10AM–6PM)* was once the resi-

dence of a prominent businessman and art collector. A short walk away, the **Picasso Museum (84)** *(Hôtel Salé, 5 rue de Thorigny, 3rd, 01-42.71.25.21, www.musee-picasso.fr; check Web site for hours)* is housed in a grand Marais mansion. Picasso admirers are treated to masterpieces in paintings, etchings, and sculptures. Kitty-corner, the **National Archives** are housed in the **Hôtel de Rohan (85)** *(87 rue Vieille-du-Temple, 3rd, 01-40.27.60.96; hours: M, W–F 10AM–12:30PM, 2PM–5:30PM, Sa–Su 2PM–5:30PM)* and around the corner in the **Hôtel de Soubise (86)** *(60 rue des Francs-Bourgeois, 3rd, 01-40.27.60.96; hours: M, W–F 10AM–12:30PM, 2PM–5:30PM, Sa–Su 2PM–5:30PM)*; both buildings are marvelous examples of 18th-century architecture. **Cloître des Billettes (87)** *(24 rue des Archives, 4th, 01-42.72.38.79, www.egliselutherienneparis.com/?q= node/22; hours: daily 11AM–7PM)*, the oldest medieval cloister in Paris, was built in 1427 for the Brothers of Charity. The courtyard, with its Gothic galleries, colonnaded arches, and arcades topped by graceful vaults, is especially appealing. The cloister presents work by emerging artists; exhibits change twice a month and are usually free. Be sure to stroll along the **rue Vieille-du-Temple (88)** *(rue de Rivoli/rue de Poitou, 3rd/4th)*—its charm comes not only from the 13th-century medieval houses but also from the street's many luxury shops. Further to the west, around **rue Ste-Croix-de-la-Bretonnerie (89)** *(rue de Temple/rue Vieille-du-Temple, 4th)*, is the gay district ("pink triangle"), a vibrant, stylish scene replete with hotels, bars, clubs, and restaurants.

Arts & Entertainment:

Magicians ply their trade outside the wonderful **Museum of Magic (90)** *(11 rue St-Paul, 4th, 01-42.72.13.26, www. museedelamagie.com; hours: W, Sa–Su 2PM–7PM)*; inside, they demonstrate with museum pieces. In a magnificent mansion, the **Maison Européenne de la Photographie (91)** *(5-7 rue de Fourcy, 4th, 01-44.78.75.00, www.mep-fr.org;*

hours: W–Su 11AM–8PM) houses more than 15,000 works of contemporary photography; and its café is super-chic. The 140-room **Musée Carnavalet (82)** *(see also page 84)* covers the history of Paris, through paintings, sculptures, documents, objects, and memorabilia. Some samplings of what is on view are: a piece of the Bastille prison, lithographs, porcelain vases, and Proust's reconstructed cork-lined bedroom (where he wrote most of *À la recherche du temps perdu, Remembrance of Things Past*). On a more human scale, the refined **Musée Cognacq-Jay (83)** *(see also page 84)* is home to a once private collection of 18th-century art and furniture. The **Picasso Museum (84)** *(see also page 84)* has an astonishing collection of work from all periods of the artist's long and diverse career. **La Galerie d'Architecture (92)** *(11 rue des Blancs-Manteaux, 4th, 01-49.96.64.00, www.galerie-architecture.fr; hours: Tu–Sa 11AM–7PM)* shows the work of contemporary architects against a clean, crisp, white backdrop.

PLACES TO EAT & DRINK
Where to Eat:

Le Pas-Sage Obligé (93) (€–€€) *(29 rue du Bourg-Tibourg, 4th, 01-40.41.95.03, www.lepassageoblige.com; hours: daily 12PM–2:30PM, 7PM–10:30PM)* ranges from vegetarian dishes to steaks and cheeseburgers. Supposedly the first wine bar in Paris, **Le Coude Fou (94) (€–€€)** *(12 rue du Bourg-Tibourg, 4th, 01-42.77.15.16, www.le coudefou.com; hours: daily 12PM–1AM)* is friendly and intimate, with food better than the usual wine bar fare. The best afternoon tea outside London is to be had at **Mariage Frères (95) (€–€€)** *(30 rue du Bourg-Tibourg,*

4th, 01-42.72.28.11, www.mariagefreres.com; hours: daily 12PM–6:30PM, tea counters & museum daily 10:30AM–7:30PM). A gem of haute cuisine, **L'Ambroisie (96) (€€€€)** (9 pl. des Vosges, 4th, 01-42.78.51.45, www.ambroisie-paris.com; hours: Tu–Sa 12PM–1:30PM, 8PM–9:30PM, closed Feb & end Jul–end Aug) is said to be one of the most beautiful restaurants in Paris. The food is spectacular while the décor is ornate and Versailles-like; the unique experience is worth the steep price. At **Au Bourguignon du Marais (97) (€€)** (52 rue François-Miron, 4th, 01-48.87.15.40; hours: Tu–Th 11:30AM–11PM, F–Sa 11:30AM–11:30PM) the excellent selection of burgundy goes with its classic bistro fare. Best for cakes and teas, **Le Loir dans la Théière (98) (€)** (3 rue des Rosiers, 4th, 01-42.72.90.61; hours: M–F 10AM–7:30PM, Sa–Su 9:30AM–7:30PM) is funky and cool; inspired by *Alice in Wonderland*, its name means "The Dormouse in the Teapot." While the Jewish character of **rue des Rosiers** may be on the wane, the African soul of nearby **rue Elzévir** is flourishing. Senegalese and African dishes and delicacies are on the menu at **Le Petit Dakar (99) (€)** (6 rue Elzévir, 3rd, 01-44.59.34.74, www.petit-dakar.abcsalles. com; hours: Tu–Su 12PM–2:30PM, 7PM–10:30PM, closed Aug); try the silky palm hearts and sweet-and-sour chicken and lemon stew. For arguably the best couscous in Paris, try **Chez Omar (100) (€€)** (47 rue de Bretagne, 3rd, 01-42.72.36.26; hours: M–Sa 12PM–2:30PM, 7PM–11:30PM, Su 7PM–11:30PM), a North African favorite among the cognoscenti. The combination

Maghreb-French cuisine is worth the wait in line. Follow the crowds waiting to get the best falafel in Paris at **L'As du Fallafel (101)** (€) *(34 rue des Rosiers, 4th, 01-48.87.63.60; hours: Su–Th 11AM–12AM, F 11AM–5PM).*

Bars & Nightlife:

You might expect Edith Piaf to saunter into **Le Connétable (102)** *(55 rue des Archives, 3rd, 01-42.77. 41.40; hours: M–F 11:15AM–3PM, 7PM–4AM, Sa–Su 7PM–4AM; daily sets 8:30PM & 10:30PM)*: it's a typical Parisian bar, chatty regulars and all. Vibrant sounds in music—from cabaret to jazz to fusion—emanate from **Les 7 Lézards (103)** *(10 rue des Rosiers, 4th, 01-48.87.08.97, www.7lezards.com; hours: opens 6PM, jazz sets begin 9PM).* At the literary wine bar **La Belle Hortense (104)** *(31 rue Vieille-du-Temple, 4th, 01-48.04.74.60, www.cafeine.com; hours: daily 5PM–2AM),* sip a glass of red wine and peruse a book from the window ledges. For some, wine's a game; at **L'Apparement Café (105)** *(18 rue des Coutures-St-Gervais, 3rd, 01-48.87.12.22; hours: M–Sa 12PM–2AM, Su 12:30PM–12AM)* wine goes with the game: you can play cards or a board game while sipping your *verre de rouge.* Further south in the gay district (also known as the "pink triangle"), **L'Open Café (106)** *(17 rue des Archives, 4th, 01-42.72.26.18, www.opencafe.fr; hours: Su–Th 11AM–2AM, F–Sa 11AM–4AM)* is a favorite gay café and a happening night spot. Stop by **Le Petit Fer à Cheval (107)** *(30 rue Vielle du Temple, 4th, 01-42.72.47.47; hours: daily 9AM–2AM),* "the little horseshoe," for drinks in vintage surrounds. There's some outdoor seating. Straight-friendly gay locale **Café Trésor (108)** *(5-7 rue du Trésor, 4th, 01-*

42.71.35.17) is a trendy bar on a lovely, small street; good for brunch or dinner too. **La Perle (109)** (78 rue Vieille-du-Temple, 3rd, 01-42.72.69.93; hours: daily 7AM–2AM) has the ambience of an old local bar/café and a gay/straight, blue collar/artist clientele.

WHERE TO SHOP

Julian Schnabel's art adorns the walls of the showroom loft of Tunisian-born Azzedine Alaïa (110) (7 rue de Moussy, 4th, 01-42.72.19.19), emphasizing that the sexy, form-fitting clothes are wearable art; check out the discounted styles at the nearby outlet (18 rue de la Verrerie, 4th, 01-42.72.54.97). Colorful tweeds and woolens, Audrey Hepburn-style, make Blancs Manteaux (111) (42 rue des Blancs Manteaux, 4th, 01-42.71.70.00, www.blancsmanteaux.com) a find; its wares are mostly shipped, so the shop is more of a depot. Contemporary interior decorations at Sentou Galerie (112) (29 rue François-Miron, 4th, 01-42.78.50.60, www.sentou.fr; hours: Tu–Sa 10AM–7PM) have become the new classics; you'll find cutting-edge French design here. Stroll through the 60 or so shops of antiques and bric-a-brac dealers at Village St-Paul (113) (along rue St-Paul, near rue Charlemagne, 4th, www.village-saint-paul.com; hours: Th–M 11AM–7PM). Senteurs de Fée (114) (10 rue de Sévigné, 3rd, 01-44.54.97.27, www.senteursdefee.com; hours: M 2PM–7:30PM, Tu–F 11AM–7:30PM, Sa 12PM–8PM) stocks incense.

Rue des Francs-Bourgeois is a great shopping street. Ekyog (115) (23 rue des Francs-Bourgeois, 4th, 01-42.78.22.60, *www.ekyog.com*; hours: *M 2PM–7PM, Tu–Sa 10:30AM–7:30PM, Su 12:30PM–7:30PM*) offers environmentally-responsible fashions in hip, chic styles. Enter Ali Baba's cave, full of fabulous Tunisian homeware, at 2 Mille et 1 Nuits (116) (*13 rue des Francs-Bourgeois, 4th, 01-48.87.07.07, 2001nuits.free.fr; hours: daily 11AM–7:30PM*). Zadig & Voltaire (117) (*42 rue des Francs-Bourgeois, 3rd, 01-44.54.00.60, www.zadig-et-voltaire. com*), with branches around the city, is popular for its casual, urban wardrobe offerings. Barbara Bui (118) (*43 rue des Francs-Bourgeois, 4th, 01-53.01.88.05, www. barbarabui.com; hours: M 12:30PM–7PM, Tu–Sa 10:30AM–7PM, Su 1PM–7PM*) reflects her French and Vietnamese roots with refined and graceful designer clothes. If the beautiful wood paneling of Dammann Frères (119) (*15 pl. des Vosges, 4th, 01-44.54.04.88, www.boutique-dammann.fr; hours: daily 11AM–7PM*) doesn't warm you, the selection of teas certainly will.

Photo buffs will flock to fashion photography bookshop Comptoir de l'Image (120) (*44 rue de Sévigné, 3rd, 01-42.72.09.17*) and Galerie Chez Valentin (121) (*9 rue St-Gilles, 3rd, 01-48.87.42.55, www.galeriechezvalentin. com; hours: Tu–Sa 11AM–1PM, 2PM–7PM*), which  exhibits experimental video, photography, and installations. African art and crafts are on display at La Boutique de la CSAO (122) (*9 rue Elzévir, 3rd, 01-42.71.33.17, www.csao.fr; hours: Tu–Sa 11AM–7PM, Su 2PM–7PM*), and contemporary African art at La Galerie 3A (123) (*9 bis rue Elzévir, 3rd, 01-42.77.66.42,*

www.csao.fr; hours: Tu–Sa 11AM–7PM, Su 2PM–7PM). Wispy fabrics, inventive details, and incredible use of color have given the Japanese fashion designer Tsumori Chisato (124) *(20 rue Barbette, 3rd, 01-42.78.18.88, www.tsumori chisato.com)* a dedicated fan base in Paris. The Bains du Marais (125) *(31-33 rue des Blancs-Manteaux, 4th, 01-44.61.02.02, www.lesbains dumarais.fr)* offers a break from the wear and tear of sightseeing and shopping. Open to women Monday through Wednesday *(M 10AM–8PM, Tu 10AM–11PM, W 10AM–7PM)*; open to men Thursday and Friday *(Th 10AM–11PM, F 10AM–8PM)*; and open to both on Wednesday evenings and weekends *(W 7PM–11PM, Sa 10AM–8PM, Su 10AM–11PM)*, the spa gives divine hammam treatments. Or you can combine a facial with manicure, pedicure, haircut, or another salon offering.

Rue Vieille-du-Temple (88) *(see also page 85)* is another treasure trove for shopping. With clothing by up-and-coming avant-garde designers, graffiti-filled walls, and photo exhibits, Surface to Air Boutique (126) *(108 rue Vieille-du-Temple, 3rd, 01–44.61.76.27, www.surface toair.com; hours: M–Sa 11:30AM–7:30PM, Su 1:30PM–7:30PM)* is the cat's meow in concept stores. Hunt for great discounts at L'Habilleur (127) *(44 rue de Poitou, 3rd, 01-48.87.77.12; hours: M–Sa 12PM–7:30PM)*: end-of-line designer pieces and hot-off-the-runway creations are 50%–70% off. Rue Charlot (128) *(beginning at rue des Quatre Fils, 3rd)* has been inventively redone, harboring galleries, bookshops, cafés, and shops, such as **Passage de Retz** *(No. 9, 01-48.04.37.99, www.passagederetz.com; hours: Tu–Su 10AM–7PM)*, **Moon Young Hee** *(No. 62, 01-48.04.39.78)*, and **Galerie Charlot** *(No. 47, 01-42.76.02.67, www.galeriecharlot. com; hours: Tu–Sa 1:30PM–6:30PM, Th til 9:30PM)*. You'll find women's wear at **Inès de la Fressange (129)** *(18 rue Commines, 3rd, 01-56.88.34.00)* (she's the official face of France, traditionally called "Marianne").

WHERE TO STAY

Hôtel Bourg Tibourg (130) *(€€€)* *(19 rue du Bourg-Tibourg, 4th, 01-42.78.47.39, www.bourgtibourg. com)*—part of the Costes Brothers' empire—is dramatic, sensual, and intimate; silk and taffeta, fringes and tassels, the hotel is a tasteful combination of styles, textures, and colors reminiscent of the private inner chambers of a princely retreat. A revamped 17th-century town house, **Hôtel de la Bretonnerie (131)** *(€–€€)* *(22 rue Ste-Croix-de-la-Bretonnerie, 4th, 01-48.87.77.63, www.bretonnerie. com)* is comfortable, tasteful, and a good value. In the budget category, **Hôtel de Nice (132)** *(€–€€)* *(42 bis, rue de Rivoli, 4th, 01-42.78.55.29, www.hoteldenice.com)* is filled with "busy" patterns and textiles and has its space challenges, but is a good bargain and is well located.

Near the Jewish quarter at the **Hôtel Caron de Beaumarchais (133)** *(€–€€)* *(12 rue Vieille-du-Temple, 4th, 01-42.72.34.12, www.carondebeaumarchais.com)* the service is impeccable; small rooms with 18th-century décor are prepared with great attention to detail. A good find at a reasonable price (especially for the neighbor-hood), **Grand Hôtel Malher (134)** *(€€)* *(5 rue Malher, 4th,*

01-42.72.60.92, www.grandhotelmalher.com) is comfortable and well run.

Simple and unassuming, **Hôtel Jeanne d'Arc (135)** (€) *(3 rue Jarente, 4th, 01-48.87.62.11, hoteljeannedarc.com)* is a great budget hotel. Modern and medieval, the luxury hotel **Pavillon de la Reine (136)** (€€€€) *(28 pl. des Vosges, 3rd, 01-40.29.19.19, www.pavillon-de-la-reine.com/uk)* has breathtaking views. Small is beautiful at **Hôtel de la Place des Vosges (137)** (€-€€) *(12 rue de Birague, 4th, 01-42.72.60.46, www.hotelplacedesvosges.com),* and accommodations are well maintained; the remodeled rooms have hardwood floors, wooden beams, and exposed stone walls (ask for the "discovery rate" for roughly a 25% discount on the new rooms). Close by, **Hôtel Turenne Le Marais (138)** (€€) *(6 rue de Turenne, 4th, 01-42.78.43.25, www.turennemarais.com)* is part of a hotel chain; rooms are color coordinated and charming. Nearer the **Musée Carnavalet (82)** and **Picasso Museum (84)**, **Hostellerie du Marais (139)** (€€) *(30 rue de Turenne, 3rd, 01-42.72.73.47, www.hostelleriedumarais.com)* has small but comfortable rooms. If you love Christian Lacroix clothes, you'll love the profusion of color in his room designs at **Hôtel du Petit Moulin (140)** (€€-€€€) *(29/31 rue de Poitou, 3rd, 01-42.74.10.10, www.hotelpetitmoulinparis.com).*

chapter 4

BASTILLE
CANAL ST-MARTIN

BASTILLE
CANAL ST-MARTIN

Places to See:

1. Place de la Bastille
2. Colonne de Juillet
3. Opéra Bastille
4. Marché d'Aligre
5. Pavillon de l'Arsenal
36. Rue du Faubourg-du-Temple
37. St-Louis Hospital
38. Port de l'Arsenal

Places to Eat & Drink:

6. Le Train Bleu
7. Le Viaduc Café
8. Le Square Trousseau
9. La Gazzetta
10. Chez Ramulaud
11. Le Temps au Temps
12. L'Ecailler du Bistrot
13. Le Bistrot Paul Bert
14. Au Vieux Chêne
15. Pause Café
16. Le Souk
17. Le Villaret
18. Le Balajo
19. Le Café du Passage
20. La Muse Vin
21. Le China

22. Café de l'Industrie
23. Le Petit Bal Perdu
39. Chez Prune
40. La Marine
41. Favela Chic
42. Le Chateaubriand
43. Hôtel du Nord
44. Le Verre Volé
45. L'Atmosphère

Where to Shop:

24. Viaduc des Arts
25. Isabel Marant
26. Gaëlle Barré
27. Anne Willi
28. Come On Eileen
29. Serge Amoruso
46. Artazart
47. Antoine et Lili

Where to Stay:

30. Hôtel Original Paris
31. Daval Hôtel
32. Hôtel le Pavillon Bastille
33. Maison Zen
34. Hôtel Gabriel
35. Hôtel de Nevers

BASTILLE

1 **5** **8** *to Bastille;* **8** *to Ledru-Rollin;*
1 **⑭** *to Gare de Lyon;* **5** **9** *to Oberkampf*

• SNAPSHOT •

The Bastille prison stormed by the people on July 14, 1789, during the French Revolution, no longer exists, though pieces of it can be seen in the Musée Carnavalet *(see Chapter 3, page 84)*. However, its ghosts seem to hover over the quarter, reminding us of the power of the people. The Place de la Bastille became a marker dividing central Paris from the working-class neighborhoods in the eastern part of the city. Now gentrified, the Bastille district has become a center of activity, from the Opéra Bastille to the burgeoning cafés and shops. Bistros and restaurants abound; many retain their working-class flavor with a twist while others bring in a new air.

PLACES TO SEE
Landmarks:

The French Revolution was followed decades later by other revolts. To commemorate those killed during the uprisings of 1830 and 1848, a bronze column was

erected in the center of the **Place de la Bastille (1)** *(bd. Beaumarchais/rue du Faubourg, 4th)*: the **Colonne de Juillet (2)** *(pl. de la Bastille, 4th)* bears the names of many buried in the crypt beneath the column. At its apex is the statue *The Genius of Liberty*. The **Opéra Bastille (3)** *(Pl. de la Bastille, 12th, box office: 120 rue de Lyon, 12th, 08-92.89.90.90, from U.S. 011-33-1-71.25.24.23, www.operadeparis.fr; box office hours: M–Sa 2:30PM–6:30PM; box office phone hours: M–F 9AM–6PM, Sa 9AM–1PM)*, officially opened by President Mitterand on Bastille Day 1989 as part of the celebrations of the Bicentennial of the French Revolution, is as far removed from the Opéra Garnier as imaginable yet still retains a majesty of its own. The façade is glass while the interior is granite with an amazing glass ceiling. A feat of technological innovation, it houses five movable stages. At the opposite end of the spectrum, the nearby **Marché d'Aligre (4)** *(pl. d'Aligre, 12th, marchedaligre.free.fr; hours: stalls, Tu–Sa 8AM–1PM, Su 8AM–2PM; covered market & shops, Tu–Sa 8AM–1PM, 4PM–7:30PM, Su 8AM–1PM)*, a frolicking food market with secondhand antique stalls, embodies the working-class character of the area.

Arts & Entertainment:

In addition to its opera season, **Opéra Bastille (3)** *(see also above)* offers free lunchtime events ("Casse-Croûte à l'Opéra") every

Thursday. The **Pavillon de l'Arsenal (5)** *(21 bd. Morland, 4th, 01-42.76.33.97, www.pavillon-arsenal.com; hours: Tu–Sa 10:30AM–6:30PM, Su 11AM–7PM)*, in an old 19th-century iron and glass warehouse, covers the urban development and architectural history of Paris through

photos, descriptions, and scale models; in individual video booths you can watch any of 120 films about Paris's architects and their work, or watch a film about the city in the video lounge. You can also catch one of the temporary exhibits of big names in architecture. Check out exhibits of contemporary artists at galleries in **rue de Charonne**, **rue de Lappe**, and **rue Keller**.

PLACES TO EAT & DRINK
Where to Eat:

At **Le Train Bleu (6)** (€€-€€€) *(pl. Louis Armand, 12th, inside Gare de Lyon train station, 1st Floor, opp. F platforms, 01-43.43.09.06, www.le-train-bleu.com; hours: daily 11:30AM–3PM, 7PM–11PM, book ahead)* ambience is everything: the murals and frescoed ceilings of this fabulous Belle-Époque brasserie will transport you. It's OK to have just a glass of champagne and stare at the walls. The Bastille area is surrounded by good, affordable bistros, once the staple of working-class life and now destinations for trendy aficionados and locals alike. **Le Viaduc Café (7)** (€€-€€€) *(43 ave. Daumesnil, 12th, 01-44.74.70.70, www.leviaduc-cafe.com; hours: daily 8AM–2AM, food served 12PM–3:30PM, 7PM–11PM)*, under the renovated railroad viaduct, is pretty and noisy, with lots of pavement tables; best for its Sunday jazz brunch. Put together fabulous Belle-Époque décor, creative cuisine, and a rising neighborhood chic factor, and you get supermodels and other celebs swarming to **Le Square Trousseau (8)** (€€) *(1 rue Antoine Vollon, 12th, 01-43.43.06.00, www.square trousseau.com; hours: daily 8AM–2AM)*. For surprising food pairings, **La Gazzetta (9)** (€–€€) *(29 rue de Cotte, 12th, 01-43.47.47.05, lagazzetta.fr; hours: Tu–Sa 12PM–3PM, 7PM–11PM)* delights: lobster in a grassy celery and lychee broth, Pyrénées lamb smothered in Jerusalem artichokes, prunes, and coffee. Art Deco accents and a tiled mosaic floor create an intriguing atmosphere; you can almost feel the ghost of Bogie hovering. The stylishness of **Chez Ramulaud (10)** (€€) *(269 rue Faubourg-St-Antoine, 11th, 01-43.72.23.29, www.chez-ramulaud.fr; hours: M–Sa 12PM–3PM, 7PM–2AM, Su 9AM–5PM, 7PM–11PM)* has contributed to its growing popularity; pols and activists are among the clientele. Three restaurants stand out in **rue Paul-Bert** for consistently good food, excellent wine, and great atmosphere: **Le Temps au Temps (11)** (€–€€) *(13 rue Paul-Bert, 11th, 01-43.79.63.40; hours: Tu–Sa, 12PM–1:30PM, 7:30PM–10:30PM, closed Aug)*, small and cozy with good contemporary cuisine; **L'Ecailler du Bistrot (12)** (€–€€) *(22 rue Paul-Bert, 11th, 01-43.72.76.77; hours: Tu–Sa 12PM–2:30PM, 7:30PM–11PM, closed Aug)*, maybe the best fish and seafood bistro in Paris, famous for its oysters; and **Le Bistrot Paul Bert (13)** (€€) *(18 rue Paul-Bert, 11th, 01-43.72.24.01; hours: Tu–Sa 12PM–2PM, 7:30PM–11PM, closed Aug)*, old-fashioned and simple, with generous portions and an owner who'll talk about wine at the drop of a hat. Recalling the 1930s, **Au Vieux Chêne (14)** (€€) *(7 rue Dahomey, 11th, 01-43.71.67.69, www.vieuxchene.fr; hours: M–F 12PM–2PM, 8PM–10:30PM, closed last week of July & first two weeks of Aug)* is a handsome bistro that's just the right fit for your antiquing expedition.

Pause Café (15) (€–€€) *(41 rue de Charonne, 11th, 01-48.06.80.33; hours: M–Sa 8AM–2AM, Su 9AM–8PM)* is welcoming with lots of outdoor seating; try the tomato and cucumber soup, and chicken sautéed in coconut milk and basil. Those trendsetters and rockers love the couscous at **Le Souk (16)** (€–€€) *(1 rue Keller, 11th, 01-49.29.05.08; hours: Tu–F 7:30PM–11:30PM, Sa 11:30AM–2:30PM, 7:30PM–12:30AM, Su 11:30AM–2:30PM, 7:30PM–11:30PM)*; you might admire the covered bazaar ambience of this Moroccan restaurant. **Le Villaret (17)** (€€) *(13 rue Ternaux, 11th, 01-43.57.89.76; hours: M–F 12:15PM–2:15PM, 7:30PM–11:30PM, Sa 7:30PM–12AM, closed Aug)* is a fabulous neighborhood bistro with creative renditions of classic French cuisine; the crowds you're likely to find there will have a mix of wine connoisseurs, neighborhood old hats, and a sprinkling of hipsters.

Bars & Nightlife:

The oldest *musette* dance hall in Paris, **Le Balajo (18)** *(9 rue de Lappe, 11th, 01-47.00.07.87, www.balajo.fr; open M–Sa, times vary, call for hours)* has an old-fashioned atmosphere that appeals, with 1950s, 1960s, 1970s music, salsa, and disco on varying nights. Come before the gig, and you can take a dancing class. **Rue de Charonne** is full of cafés and wine bars. The relaxed, romantic **Le Café du Passage (19)** *(12 rue de Charonne, 11th, 01-49.29.97.64;*

hours: M–F 6PM–2AM, Sa 6PM–12AM) offers more than 300 wines of great vintages. **La Muse Vin (20)** *(101 rue de Charonne, 11th, 01-40.09.93.05; hours: M–Sa 11AM–12AM)* is a "natural" wine bar (organic wine made without industrial additives), with wines mostly unknown in the U.S. (beware the heavy cigarette smoke). Atmospheric **Le China (21)** *(50 rue de Charenton, 12th, 01-43.46.08.09, www.lechina.eu; hours: M–F 12PM–2AM, Sa–Su 5PM–2AM)* makes cocktail hour exotic. Of the plentiful cool cafés around the Bastille, **Café de l'Industrie (22)** *(16 rue St-Sabin, 11th, 01-47.00.13.53; hours: daily 9AM–12AM)*, a local haunt, is cheery and friendly. Another throwback to the 1960s, **Le Petit Bal Perdu (23)** *(25 rue Oberkampf, 11th, 01-48.06.28.23; hours: M–F 11AM–2AM, Sa 5PM–2AM)* is a friendly local bar and restaurant with a jukebox.

WHERE TO SHOP

Renovated and glassed in, the arcades of an old railway viaduct house the Viaduc des Arts (24) *(1-129 ave. Daumesnil, 12th, 01-44.75.80.66, www.viaducdesarts.fr; check Web site for hours)*, with its craft shops, galleries, exhibition spaces, and open *ateliers* where artisans weave and hammer, stitch and iron. Notable among them: **Cécile et Jeanne** *(No. 49, 01-43.41.60.84)*, with jewelry and handbags; **VIA** *(Valorisation de l'Innovation dans l'Ameublement, Nos. 29–35, 01-46.28.11.11)*, exhibiting textiles, furniture, and home accessories; **Home Intra** *(No. 47, 01-44.75.34.34)*, with home furnishings, drapes, tapestries, and upholstering to order or ready-made; **Série Rare** *(No. 121, 01-55.42.92.10)* for fabulous bronze doorknobs, tie-backs, and other architectural fittings inspired by antiquity; and **Jean-Charles Brosseau** *(No. 129, 01-53.33.82.00)*, designer *extraordinaire* of perfumes and hats. There are real "finds" among the second-hand merchandise at the **Marché d'Aligre (4)** *(see also page 97)*. Isabel Marant (25) *(16 rue de Charonne, 11th, 01-49.29.71.55, www.isabelmarant.tm.fr; hours: M 11AM–7PM, Tu–Sa 10:30AM–7:30PM)* designs feminine clothing in silks, cashmere, and other fine fabrics. In **rue Keller**, the seductive mohair creations of Gaëlle Barré (26) *(17 rue Keller, 11th, 01-43.14.63.02, www.gaelle barre.com; hours: Tu–Sa 11:30AM–7:30PM)* will turn your head. A few doors away, Anne Willi (27) *(13 rue Keller, 11th, 01-48.06.74.06, www.annewilli.com)* designs are elegant and versatile. With three floors of vintage delight at Come On Eileen (28) *(16-18 rue des Taillandiers, 11th, 01-43.38.12.11; hours: M–Sa 11AM–8:30PM, Su 2PM–8PM)*, pieces range from funky cowboy duds to Hermès scarves. The handmade leather goods at Serge Amoruso (29) *(13 rue Abel, 12th, 01-43.40.83.66; call for hours)* are a labor of love; watch the artisans as they perform magic in the workshop.

WHERE TO STAY

The former Hôtel Lyon-Mulhouse has been reborn as **Hôtel Original Paris (30)** (€–€€) *(8 bd. Beaumarchais, 11th, 01-47.00.91.50, www.hoteloriginalparis.com)*, with a fresh, quirky, and colorful new decor. Functional rooms with A/C and access to the galleries, cafés, and boutiques of the area make **Daval Hôtel (31)** (€) *(21 rue Daval, 11th, 01-47.00.51.23, www.hoteldaval.com)* a good budget choice. A hop away from the Opéra Bastille, **Hôtel le Pavillon Bastille (32)** (€-€€) *(65 rue de Lyon, 12th, 01-43.43.65.65, www.paris-hotel-pavillonbastille.com)* is bright and cheery, with small but comfortable rooms and baths, a young, friendly staff, and a charming courtyard. Recent renovations include A/C and soundproofing. Or consider a studio apartment at the **Maison Zen (33)** (€-€€) *(35 rue de Lyon, 12th, 01-77.11.13.36, www.maison zen.com, cheap weekly rates, credit cards not accepted)*; sunny, whitewashed units with Ikea furnishings surround a tree-lined cobblestone courtyard. Modern rooms at **Hôtel Gabriel (34)** (€-€€) *(25 rue du Grand Prieuré, 11th, 01-47.00.13.38, www.gabriel parismarais.com)* have minimalist lines with soothing colors and a NightCove® apparatus that helps ensure restful sleep through light and sound programs. The hotel also proposes various detox options, from organic breakfasts to antioxidant drinks. If detox drinks aren't your thing, alcoholic varieties are offered as well. The Detox Room provides massages and skincare treatments by appointment. A very cheap sleep will rescue the budget weary at **Hôtel de Nevers (35)** (€) *(53 rue de Malte, 11th, 01-47.00.56.18, www.hoteldenevers.fr)*; it's clean but furnishings consist basically of a bed only, and bathrooms are shared.

CANAL ST-MARTIN

③ ⑤ ⑧ ⑨ ⑪ *to République;*
⑤ *to Jacques Bonsergent;* ② *to Colonel Fabien;*
⑦ *to Château Landon or Louis Blanc;*
② ⑤ ⑦ᵇⁱˢ *to Jaurès;* ② ⑤ ⑦ *to Stalingrad*

• SNAPSHOT •

With Marais rents soaring, emerging designers, artists, and media start-ups are moving northward to the increasingly hip and bohemian Canal St-Martin. Overwhelmingly for the young (20- and 30-some-things), the area is fast becoming the "in" place. Its less frenetic pace gives it a village atmosphere with urban sophistication. The three-mile canal, a Seine shortcut, is fascinating to observe as boats maneuver adroitly through locks and under bridges.

PLACES TO SEE
Landmarks:

From the **Place de la République** all the way up to the end of the canal at **Bassin de la Villette**, the working-class underpinnings of the Canal St-Martin area are evident. The houses, taverns, cafés, warehouses, and factories all reveal aspects of that 19th-century world. In the **rue du Faubourg-du-Temple (36)** *(starting at pl. de la République, 10th)*, a busy street full of ethnic shops and restaurants, details on some buildings and storefronts testify to the care taken in embellishing this working-class neighborhood. However, even the 17th-century **St-Louis Hospital (37)** *(1 ave. Claude-Vellefaux, 10th, 01-42.49.49.49, www.chustlouis.fr)*, beautiful though it is, has none of the luxurious ornamentation of the more aristocratic Right Bank districts bordering the river. The best way to see the area is to take a **boat trip** up the canal, passing under romantic footbridges and through its nine locks: you board a Canauxrama boat at **Port de l'Arsenal (38)** *(opposite 50 bd. de la Bastille, 12th, 01-42.39.15.00 for a 3-hour ride; see Bastille neighborhood on the map; at northern end of canal, board at Bassin de la Villette, 13 quai de la Loire, 19th, 01-42.39.15.00, www.canauxrama.com)*. Alternatively, walking along the **Quai de Valmy** or **Quai de Jemmapes** is a relaxed way of absorbing young, cutting-edge Paris and the making of chic.

PLACES TO EAT & DRINK
Where to Eat:

With the Canal St-Martin attracting converts, "funk" is in and **Chez Prune (39)** (€) *(71 quai de Valmy/36 rue Beaurepaire, 10th, 01-42.41.30.47; hours: M–Sa 8AM–2AM, Su 10AM–2AM)* has become a prime example of a trendy café-bar. Eclectic and unpretentious, its strongest appeal is the view over the canal on the **Quai de Valmy**. Another café popular in this youthful neighborhood is **La Marine (40)** (€–€€) *(55 bis, quai de Valmy, 10th, 01-42.39.69.81; hours: M–F 7:30AM–2AM, Sa–Su 8:30AM–2AM)*.

The Brazilian home-style food at **Favela Chic (41)** (€-€€) (*18 rue du Faubourg-du-Temple, 11th, 01-40.21.38.14, www.favelachic.com; hours: Tu–Sa 8PM–12AM*), mixed with irresistible music, will have you dancing between courses. **Le Chateaubriand (42)** (€€€) (*129 ave. Parmentier, 11th, 01-43.57.45.95, www.lechateaubriand.net; hours: Tu–Sa 7:30PM–8:30PM with reservations, from 9:30PM without reservations*) has been rated among the best restaurants in the world by chefs and food critics. The colorful cuisine mixes raw and cooked ingredients in a fantasy of tastes. Romantic **Hôtel du Nord (43)** (€-€€) (*102 quai de Jemmapes, 10th, 01-40.40.78.78, www.hoteldunord.org; hours: restaurant daily 12PM–3PM, 8PM–12AM; café daily 9AM–1:30AM*), where the 1938 film of the same name was shot, is an idyllic spot overlooking a footbridge of the canal. In the evenings it swings with live music.

Bars & Nightlife:

Tiny and simple, **Le Verre Volé (44)** (*67 rue de Lancry, 10th, 01-48.03.17.34, www.leverrevole.fr; call for hours*) is a combination wine bar, bistro, and wine shop. Off **Quai de Valmy**, the eclectic bar **L'Atmosphère (45)** (*49 rue Lucien-Sampaix, 10th, 01-40.38.09.21, www.latmosphere.fr; hours: 10AM–12AM*) has seating outdoors along the canal, which allows you to soak up the atmosphere, and live music Sunday afternoons. **Hôtel du Nord (43)** (*see also above; entertainment reservations, 01-40.40.78.78*) features live jazz Wednesday nights, cabaret songs Fridays, and a singer Saturdays. Twice a month, comedy is performed in English.

LATIN QUARTER
ÎLE DE LA CITÉ
ÎLE ST-LOUIS

Places to See:

1. Place St-Michel
2. Shakespeare & Co.
3. St-Julien-le-Pauvre
4. St-Séverin
5. National Museum of the Middle Ages (Cluny Museum)
6. Sorbonne
7. Collège de France
8. Panthéon
9. Place de la Contrescarpe
10. Rue Mouffetard
11. Paris Mosque
12. Jardin des Plantes
13. National Museum of Natural History
14. Arènes de Lutèce
15. Institute of the Arab World
58. Square du Vert-Galant
59. Palais de Justice
60. SAINTE-CHAPELLE ★
61. Conciergerie
62. Flower and Bird Market
63. Crypte Archéologique
64. NOTRE-DAME ★
65. Memorial of the Deportation
67. Hôtel Chenizot
68. Hôtel Lambert
69. St-Louis-en-l'Ile

Places to Eat & Drink:

16. La Fourmi Ailée
17. Le Reminet
18. L'Atelier Maître Albert
19. Le Pré Verre
20. Brasserie Balzar
21. ChantAirelle
22. Le Berthoud
23. Le Cosi
24. Le Perraudin
25. Café de la Nouvelle Mairie
26. Les Cinq Saveurs d'Anada
27. Bonjour Vietnam
28. L'Assiette aux Fromages
29. Vegan Folie's
30. Le Jardin des Pâtes
31. La Nouvelle Vie
32. Au Moulin à Vent
33. La Tour d'Argent
34. La Rôtisserie du Beaujolais
35. Inagiku
36. Caveau de la Huchette
37. Caveau des Oubliettes
38. Café Egyptien

★ *Top Picks*

LATIN QUARTER

4 to St-Michel;
10 to Cluny-La Sorbonne or Maubert-Mutualité;
7 to Censier-Daubentonn or Place Monge;
7 10 to Jussieu; **10** to Cardinal Lemoine

• SNAPSHOT •

The Latin Quarter is the student district where Paris's first university, the Sorbonne, was founded in 1253. At the time, Latin was the language of scholars; thus the area acquired its name. Still buzzing with students and full of different ethnic influences, the Latin Quarter, though commercial and touristy, remains bohemian, vibrant, and full of young people. Although the echoes of the famous 1968 student/worker strike have long faded, the inexpensive shops, ethnic boutiques, avant-garde theatres, and cinemas remain, as do vestiges of much earlier times. Around Boulevard St-Michel, the main street, is a labyrinth of cobblestoned passages, and the rue St-Jacques, an old Roman road, is the precursor of all Parisian streets. The Latin Quarter and its eastern flank, Jussieu, are full of interesting museums, from the magnificent medieval Cluny Museum to the breathtaking Institute of the Arab World with its modern architectural design based on age-old Islamic motifs. Even the Jardin des Plantes, one of Paris's great parks, includes a

zoo, botanical school, and the natural history museum and study center, in keeping with the Latin Quarter's centuries-old dedication to culture and learning.

PLACES TO SEE
Landmarks:

At the north end of the busy Boulevard St-Michel, or "Boul'Mich," its nickname, is the **Place St-Michel (1)**, with its ornately sculpted fountain. The site of Paris Commune uprisings in 1871 and student unrest in May 1968, it is now a common meeting point for students. The square borders the river, facing the Pont St-Michel bridge. A stroll along these quays of the Seine is a must: they're filled with the famous bookstalls, the **bouquinistes**. Around the corner from Place St-Michel, along the quay, is **Shakespeare & Co. (2)** *(37 rue de la Bûcherie, 5th, 01-43.25.40.93, www.shakespeareandcompany.com; hours: M–F 10AM–11PM, Sa–Su 11AM–11PM)*, the chaotic but cozy bookstore famous for the stream of literati who've passed through its doors. Nearby, the church of **St-Julien-le-Pauvre (3)** *(1 rue St-Julien-le-Pauvre or 79 rue Galande, 5th, 01-43.54.52.16, www.sjlpmelkites.fr)*, now Greek Orthodox, is one of the oldest in Paris. A short, narrow

street in this area, the **rue Galande**, is synonymous with notorious taverns. A few cobbled streets away, the Flamboyant Gothic church **St-Séverin (4)** *(1-3 rue des Prêtres-St-Séverin, 5th, 01-42.34.93.50, www.saint-severin. com; hours: M–Sa 11AM–7:30PM, Su 9AM–8:30PM)* flaunts its beauty with spires, balustrades, and gargoyles.

Perhaps the jewel of the Latin Quarter is the **National Museum of the Middle Ages (5)** *(6 pl. Paul-Painlevé, 5th, 01-53.73.78.00/16, www.musee-moyenage.fr; hours: W–M 9:15AM–5:45PM)*, often referred to by its previous name, the Cluny Museum. A unique combination of Gallo-Roman ruins, baths dating from A.D. 200, and a medieval mansion built by the Abbot of Cluny in 1500, the museum affords the traveler a trip into history, in both its ambience and its collection.

The **Sorbonne (6)** *(47 rue des Écoles, 5th, 01-40.46. 22.11, www.sorbonne.fr; hours: M–F 9AM–5PM)*, seat of the 13 autonomous University of Paris branches and a world-famous institution of learning, has produced some of the most important intellectuals in history. In the main courtyard, the **Chapel of the Sorbonne** is a monument to Richelieu. Across the street is the research institute **Collège de France (7)** *(11 pl. Marcelin-Berthelot, 5th, 01-44.27.12.11, www.college-de-france.fr; hours: library M–F 10AM–6PM)*, founded in 1530.

A few streets south is the **Panthéon (8)** *(pl. du Panthéon, 5th, 01-44.32.18.00, www.pantheon.monuments-nationaux.fr; hours: Apr–Sep daily 10AM–6:30PM, Oct–Mar daily 10AM–6PM)*, originally designed to be an 18th-century neoclassical church, which was built by Louis XV. After surviving a terrible illness, he wanted to give thanks, so he dedicated the building to the patron saint of Paris, Sainte Geneviève; murals telling her story line its interior walls. After the French Revolution, it was turned into a pantheon, the crypt of great figures of France: Voltaire, Jean-Jacques Rousseau, Émile Zola, Victor Hugo, Pierre and Marie Curie, Jean Moulin, and Jean Monnet, father of the European Community, are entombed here.

Other prominent figures have trod the pavement of **Place de la Contrescarpe (9)** *(5th)*. This is where the 16th-century group of writers known as *La Pléiade* used to meet. Ernest Hemingway lived in **39 rue Descartes** when he was an unknown writer, then later with his wife Hadley at **74 rue du Cardinal-Lemoine.**

Today's Parisians teem in the **rue Mouffetard (10)** *(5th)*. It's one of the city's oldest thoroughfares, dating from Roman times. You can still see ancient painted signs on some shops. This pedestrian street is famous today for its open-air markets, especially in **Place Maubert**, **Place Monge**, and the adjacent **rue Daubenton**, home to an upbeat African market. Follow rue Daubenton eastward and you'll arrive at the **Paris Mosque (11)** *(2 bis, pl. du puits de l'Ermite, 5th, 01-45.35.97.33, www. mosquee-de-paris.net; call for hours and guided tours)*. Built in Hispano-Moorish style, the spiritual structure is a splendid creation incorporating decorative tiles, intricately carved lace-like wood screens, and magnificent carpets. The interior patio garden was modeled on the Alhambra in Granada. Its café serves traditional mint tea and delicious pastries. An authentic hammam is open on alternate days to men and women.

Across from the mosque, the **Jardin des Plantes (12)** *(57 rue Cuvier, 5th, 01-40.79.56.01/54.79, www.mnhn. fr; hours: summer daily 7:30PM–8PM, winter daily 8AM–5:30PM)*, Paris's botanical garden, boasts ancient trees and remarkable displays of wild and herbaceous plants. It also features a zoo, botanical school, and several galleries of the French **National Museum of Natural History (13)** *(36 rue Geoffroy St-Hilaire, 5th, 01-40.79. 54.79/56.01, www.mnhn.fr; hours: W–M 10AM–6PM)*, including galleries of evolution, minerals and geology, and paleontology and comparative anatomy. To the northwest, the **Arènes de Lutèce (14)** *(rue de Navarre/47 rue Monge, 5th, 01-45.35.02.56; hours: winter daily 8AM–5:30PM, summer daily 9AM–9:30PM)*, the remains of a Gallo-Roman arena (Romans named Paris "Lutetia"), was probably used for theatrical performances and gladiator fights, a combined use particular to Gaul. Seating 15,000, it was arranged in 35 tiers. Winding northward, you arrive at the **Institute of the Arab World (15)** *(1 rue des Fossées-St-Bernard, 5th, 01-40.51.38.38, www.imarabe. org; hours: Tu–Th 10AM–6PM, F 10AM–9:30PM, Sa–Su 10AM–7PM)*, designed by French architect Jean Nouvel. A breathtaking building that encapsulates the spirit and motifs of traditional Arab architecture using modern materials, this cultural institute and museum was founded in 1980 by France and 20 Arab nations and dedicated to nurturing cultural understanding and cooperation between the Islamic world and the West. The southern façade comprises 1,600 high-tech metal screens; modeled on Moorish screens of carved wood, they filter the sunlight entering the building.

Arts & Entertainment:

For chamber and religious music concerts, **St-Julien-le-Pauvre (3)** *(see also page 112)* is the perfect venue. English-language bookstore **Shakespeare & Co. (2)** *(see also page 112)* hosts poetry readings. The cultural wealth of the Latin Quarter lies in its museums. Besides a superb collection of illuminated manuscripts, sculptures, ceramics, woodcarvings, precious metals, and Gallo-Roman ruins, the **National Museum of the Middle Ages (5)** (also known as Cluny Museum) *(see also page 113)* is home to the famous **Lady with the Unicorn**, a series of six exquisite 15th-century tapestries, the **Gallery of the Kings**, 21 stone heads of the Kings of Judah (13th century), two **Books of Hours** (15th century), and the **Golden Rose of Basel**, a rose sculpted in gold for the Avignon Pope John XXII (14th century). Columns, a pediment relief, and a grandiose dome lend majesty to the façade of the **Panthéon (8)** *(see also page 113)*. Inside, frescoes, statues, and decorative archways are appropriate monuments in this shrine to great personages of French history. On several floors of the magnificent **Institute of the Arab World (15)** *(see also page 115)*, Islamic works of art span the 9th to 19th centuries. The lower level displays art works from the Arab world since 1950: photography, graphic arts, painting, sculpture, and calligraphy. The **National Museum of Natural History (13)** *(see also page 115)* fascinates with its exhibits of humans and animals as well as its mineralogical and gemstone displays. It's famous for its Grand Hall of Evolution.

PLACES TO EAT & DRINK
Where to Eat:

For a long, cozy lunch, **La Fourmi Ailée (16)** (€-€€) *(8 rue du Fouarre, 5th, 01-43.29.40.99, www.parisresto.com; hours: daily 12PM–12AM)* specializes in tarts; the service is slow but the library-den ambience is charming. **Le Reminet (17)** (€€) *(3 rue des Grands-Degrés, 5th, 01-44.07.04.24, www.lereminet.com; hours: daily 12PM–2:30PM, 7PM–10:30PM)* was a well-kept secret, but the word is out: the food's memorable; the service delightful. Country flair, Latin Quarter buzz, and a view of Notre-Dame add atmosphere to the classic fare at **L'Atelier Maître Albert (18)** (€€-€€€) *(1 rue Maître-Albert, 5th, 01-56.81.30.01, www.ateliermaitrealbert.com; hours: M–W 12PM–2:30PM, 6:30PM–11PM, Th, F 12PM–2:30PM, 6:30PM–1AM, Sa 6:30PM–1AM, Su 6:30PM–11PM)*. Just north of the Sorbonne, **Le Pré Verre (19)** (€€) *(8 rue Thénard, 5th, 01-43.54.59.47, www.lepreverre.com; hours: Tu–Sa 12PM–2PM, 7:30PM–10:30PM)*, a popular bistro, charming and casual, whips up inventive dishes with exotic spices, appropriate for the background jazz music. Rub elbows with Left Bank pundits at **Brasserie Balzar (20)** (€€-€€€) *(49 rue des Ecoles, 5th, 01-43.54.13.67 www.brasseriebalzar.com; hours: daily 8:30AM–11:30PM)*; it hasn't changed much since Sartre and Camus used to drop in, sawdust on the floor and all. **ChantAirelle (21)** (€-€€) *(17 rue de Laplace, 5th, 01-46.33. 18.59, www.chantairelle.com;*

hours: open to 10PM, closed Sa lunch, Su, & M dinner), with its hearty food and rustic décor, is so authentic you might think you were in the Auvergne. Romance mixes with healthy dishes at **Le Berthoud (22)** (€-€€) (*1 rue Valette, 5th, 01-43.54.38.81; hours: M–F 12PM–11PM, Sa 7PM–1AM, closed Aug*). **Le Cosi (23)** (€€) (*9 rue Cujas, 5th, 01-43.29.20.20, www.le-cosi.com; hours: M–Sa 12PM–2:45PM, 7:30PM–11:15PM*), a Corsican restaurant, is famous for its chestnut soufflé and its charming bookstore.

Restaurants around the Panthéon aren't fussy. For home-style French classics, **Le Perraudin (24)** (€€) (*157 rue St-Jacques, 5th, 01-46.33.15.75, www.restaurant-perraudin.com; open daily for lunch & dinner, call for hours*) is the real thing; so typically 1900s, down to the Turkish toilet! **Café de la Nouvelle Mairie (25)** (€-€€) (*19-21 rue des Fossés-St-Jacques, 5th, 01-44.07.04.41; hours: M–F 8AM–12AM*) is the perfect café: friendly, relaxing, with a lovely terrace.

Toward rue Mouffetard (10), **Les Cinq Saveurs d'Anada (26)** (€) (*72 rue du Cardinal-Lemoine, 5th, 01-43.29.58.54, www.anada-5-saveurs.com; hours: Tu–Su 12PM–2:30PM, 7PM–10:30PM*) serves delicious organic vegetarian dishes. **Bonjour Vietnam (27)** (€) (*6 rue Thouin, 5th, 01-43.54.78.04; hours: M–Sa 11:30AM–3PM, 6:30PM–10PM*), tiny and busy, has great *pho* and crispy spring rolls. Beware the tourist traps along rue Mouffetard (10). However, rest assured that **L'Assiette aux Fromages (28)** (€) (*25 rue Mouffetard, 5th, 01-43.36.91.59, www.lassietteauxfromages.fr; hours:*

Apr–Sep daily 12PM–12AM, Oct–Mar daily 12PM–2:30PM, 6:30PM–12AM) isn't one of them. It's all things cheese—fondue, quiches, tarts, raclette—along with great bread and salads. A good cheap eat is the bakery **Vegan Folie's (29)** (€) *(53 rue Mouffetard, 5th, 01-43.37.21.89; hours: Tu–Su 11AM–8PM)*, with great sweet and savory cupcakes; all are vegan with gluten-free choices.

Across from the Jardin des Plantes, the organic pasta at **Le Jardin des Pâtes (30)** (€) *(4 rue Lacépède, 5th, 01-43.31.50.71; hours: daily 12PM–2:30PM, 7PM–11PM)* is delicious: try the chestnut *(châtaigne)* pasta with duck fillet, mushrooms, and cream. The dishes at **La Nouvelle Vie (31)** (€) *(36 rue des Boulangers, 5th, 01-44.07.13.29; hours: M 12PM–2PM, Tu–Sa 12PM–2PM, 7PM–9:30PM, Su 7PM–9:30PM)* are memorable, from the honey and goat cheese tart to the filet of duck breast in green pepper sauce. On the other end of the spectrum, **Au Moulin à Vent (32)** (€€-€€€) *(20 rue des Fossés-St-Bernard, 5th, 01-43.54.99.37, www.au-moulinavent.com; hours: Tu–F 12PM–2:15PM, 7:30PM–11PM, Sa 7:30PM–11PM)* is known for great steaks.

Very expensive, very entrancing, and one of Paris's most fabled restaurants, **La Tour d'Argent (33)** (€€€€) *(15 quai de la Tournelle, 5th, 01-43.54.23.31, www.latourdargent. com; reservation hours: Tu–Sa 12PM–1:30PM, 7:30PM–9:30PM, closed Aug)* is high-class with a fabulous view of Notre-Dame. Its modestly-priced neighbor, **La Rôtisserie du Beaujolais (34)** (€€) *(19 quai de la Tournelle, 5th, 01-43.54.17.47; hours: daily 12PM–2:15PM, 7:30PM–*

10:15PM) has the same view and feeds bustling crowds with less fancy, but tasty, dependable classics. Try fresh seafood, sizzling in front of you on the teppanyaki grill, at **Inagiku (35) (€-€€€)** *(14 rue de Pontoise, 5th, 01-43.54.70.07, www.restaurant-inagiku.fr; hours: daily 12PM–2:30PM, 7PM–11PM).*

Bars & Nightlife:

Medieval cellars around St-Michel have turned into jazz clubs: **Caveau de la Huchette (36)** *(5 rue de la Huchette, 5th, 01-43.26.65.05, www.caveaudelahuchette.fr; hours: Su–W 9:30PM–2:30AM, Th–Sa 9:30PM–dawn)* and **Caveau des Oubliettes (37)** *(52 rue Galande, 5th, 01-46.34.23.09, www.caveaudesoubliettes.fr; hours: daily 5PM–4AM)* are on the tourist circuit, but they offer good acts. Student nightlife buzzes around **Place de la Contrescarpe (9)** *(see also page 114),* full of tiny bars and cafés. Check out **Café Egyptien (38)** *(112 rue Mouffetard, 5th, entrance on rue de l'Arbalète, 01-43.31.11.35, www.lecafeegyptien.com; hours: daily 12PM–2AM)* for Arab music, mint tea, and a midnight nosh. On Sunday evenings from June to October the **Square Tino Rossi (39)** *(5th)* on the banks of the Seine by the Jardin des Plantes fills with hip-shaking rhythm lovers dancing their feet off—rumba, mambo, tango, samba, you name it, they'll swing. Architectural artifacts from churches grace the pub **La Gueuze (40)** *(19 rue Soufflot, 5th, 01-43.54.63.00; hours: Su–Th 12PM–2AM, F–Sa 12PM–4AM)*; its selection of beers is prodigious.

WHERE TO SHOP

The Latin Quarter is full of small shops, mostly catering to students' needs and wallets. Stroll by the **bouquinistes**, the stalls along the quays of the Seine: You'll find new and old books (even first editions), prints, maps, and postcards. **Shakespeare & Co. (2)** *(see also page 112)* is the mecca for English-language book lovers. **The Abbey Bookshop (41)** *(29 rue de la Parcheminerie, 5th, 01-46.33.16.24, www.abbeybookshop.wordpress.com; hours: M–Sa 10AM–7PM)*, "a quiet refuge for poet, scholar, or pilgrim," specializes in Canadian books and authors. **Librairie Gibert Joseph (42)** *(26-34 bd. St-Michel, 6th, 01-44.41.88.88, www.gibertjoseph.com; hours: M–Sa 10AM–8PM)* stocks new and used books, CDs, and notebooks. The treasure trove of antique toys at **La Tortue Electrique (43)** *(7 rue Frédéric-Sauton, 5th, 01-43.29.37.08, www.tortueelectrique.org; hours: Tu–Sa 2PM–6PM)* will recall childhood past, while the divinely scented candles at **Diptyque (44)** *(34 bd. St-Germain, 5th, 01-43.26.77.44, www.diptyqueparis.com; hours: M–Sa 10AM–7PM)* will transport you back to France when they're burning in your home long after your trip.

Les Papilles (45) *(30 rue Gay-Lussac, 5th, 01-43.25.20.79, www.lespapillesparis.fr; hours: M–Sa open to 10PM, closed 3 wks Aug)* stocks regional French gourmet foods. It is also a restaurant, and a gourmet-lover's delight. Products from Brittany—pea coats, sweaters, striped Breton T-shirts, pottery—are the real thing at **Breiz Norway (46)** *(33 rue Gay-Lussac, 5th, 01-43.29.47.82).* For shopping or gawking, the open-air markets on **rue Mouffetard (10)** *(see also page 114)* and the African market on **rue Daubenton** afford authentic Parisian experiences. La Tuile à Loup (47) *(35 rue Daubenton, 5th, 01-47.07.28.90; www.latuilealoup.com; hours: M 1PM–6PM, Tu–Sa 10:30AM–6PM)* sells regional French table and housewares. Nearby Marché Monge (48) *(pl. Monge, 5th; hours: W, F 7AM–2:30PM, Su 7AM–3PM)*, less touristy, is full of feisty produce hawkers.

Old-world door handles and other lovely fixtures can be found at the hardware store La Quincaillerie (49) *(3-4 bd. St-Germain, 5th, 01-46.33.66.71, www.laquincaillerie. com; hours: M–F 10AM–1PM, 2PM–7PM, Sa 10AM–1PM, 2PM–6PM; accessory shop at No. 4 closed Su & M).* Comptoirs Tour d'Argent Art de la Table (50) *(2 rue du Cardinal-Lemoine, 5th, 01-46.33.45.58)*, the famous restaurant's shop, sells fine china, crystal, and silverware.

WHERE TO STAY

The rooms at Hôtel Agora St-Germain (51) (€-€€) *(42 rue des Bernardins, 5th, 01-46.34.13.00, www. AgoraSaintGermain.com)* have space, silk wallpaper, marble-tiled bathrooms, and A/C (not a given in non-luxury hotels). Located across a tree-filled square, Hôtel Résidence Henri IV (52) (€€-€€€) *(50 rue des Bernardins, 5th, 01-44.41.31.81, www.residencehenri4.com)* is quiet and comfortable; kitchenettes and lovely two-room suites are available.

Facing the Sorbonne, Grand Hôtel St-Michel (53) (€€) *(19 rue Cujas, 5th, 01-46.33.33.02, www.grand-hotel-st-michel.com)* has a sophisticated look, with spacious rooms, A/C, and hand-painted furniture. An elegant converted 18th-century town house, the **Hôtel du Panthéon (54)** (€-€€€) *(19 pl. du Panthéon, 5th, 01-43.54.32.95, www.hoteldupantheon.com)*, with its atrium garden and view of the Panthéon, is tastefully appointed with antique furniture, coordinated fabrics, and framed artwork in high-ceilinged rooms.

Familia Hôtel (55) (€) *(11 rue des Écoles, 5th, 01-43.54. 55.27, www.hotel-paris-familia.com)* is a great deal; exposed stone walls or painted murals coordinate with tapestry wall hangings. Another bargain is the **Hôtel des Grandes Écoles (56)** (€) *(75 rue du Cardinal-Lemoine, 5th, 01-43.26.79.23, www.hotel-grandes-ecoles.com)*: the terrace overlooks a garden, which will transport you to a peaceful French countryside setting after a long day of city sightseeing.

Hôtel Relais Saint-Jacques (57) (€€-€€€) *(3 rue de l'Abbé-de-l'Épée, 5th, 01-53.73.26.00, www.relais-saint-jacques.com)* is a boutique hotel inspired by the Loire Valley's châteaux; traditional décor and modern amenities create a luxurious experience.

4 to Cité or St-Michel; **1 4 7 14** to Châtelet

• SNAPSHOT •

Île de la Cité is where Paris began: around 250 B.C. a tribe of Celtic Gauls, river traders called the Parisii, settled on the island. With the river encircling it like a moat, it was easily defendable. Île de la Cité became the seat of power and the site of a royal palace (now the law courts). Monumental buildings arose: Notre-Dame Cathedral, Sainte-Chapelle, and the Conciergerie. These historical buildings lend majesty to the island and magnificence to the riverfront. Amid the enormity of its power and beauty, the island still contains pockets of smaller-scale charm.

PLACES TO SEE
Landmarks:

The western tip of the island, the tree-lined triangle of the **Square du Vert-Galant (58)** *(1st)*, named after the amorous King Henri IV, is one of the most beautiful areas of Paris. The Seine stretches out on either side; beyond the river, Paris sprawls at your feet. **Pont Neuf** ("New Bridge"), the oldest bridge in Paris, connects the island to the rest of the city. To the east is **Place Dauphine** *(1st)*, another haven of charm and calm. The **Palais de Justice (59)** *(4 bd. du Palais, 1st, 01-44.32.52.52; hours: M–F 8AM–6PM)*, now the law courts, was for centuries the royal palace, until the king moved to the Marais in the 14th century. During the French Revolution, the site became a tribunal. Nestled among the courts, **★SAINTE-CHAPELLE (60)** *(4 bd. du Palais, 1st, 01-53.40.60.80, www.monuments-nationaux.fr; hours: Mar–Oct daily 9:30AM–6PM, Nov–Feb daily 9AM–5PM; W til 9PM mid-May–mid-Sep)* is among Europe's greatest architectural masterpieces. Famous for its 15 magnificent stained-glass windows depicting more than 1,000 religious scenes, the chapel is characterized by lofty vaulted ceilings. Louis IX built the chapel in 1248 to house Christian relics, including what was purported to be Christ's crown of thorns.

To the north is the **Conciergerie (61)** *(2 bd. du Palais/1 quai de l'Horloge, 1st, 01-53.40.60.80, www.monuments-nationaux.fr; hours: daily 9:30AM–6PM)*, the prison made infamous during the Revolution. Marie Antoinette was jailed there until her execution; so were Charlotte Corday, who stabbed Revolutionary leader Marat; and Revolutionary judges Danton and Robespierre. East of the Conciergerie, the famous **Flower and Bird Market (62)** *(pl. Louis-Lépine, 4th; hours: M–Sa 8AM–7:30PM, Su 8AM–7PM)* adds a splash of life and color to an area of daunting administrative buildings. Gallo-Roman ruins and vestiges of 2,000-year-old houses are on view in the **Crypte Archéologique (63)** *(7 pl. du Parvis-Notre-Dame, 4th, 01-55.42.50.10, http://crypte.paris.fr; hours: Tu–Sa 10AM–6PM)*.

It is located on the main square of one of Paris's most famous structures, the Gothic cathedral of ★NOTRE-DAME (64) *(6 Parvis Notre-Dame de Paris, pl. Jean-Paul II, 4th, 01-42.34.56.10, www.notredamedeparis.fr; hours: M–F 8AM–6:45PM, Sa–Su 8AM–7:15PM).* It took 170 years to build

this magnificent cathedral, which was pillaged during the French Revolution and later restored. The heads of the façade's 28 statues of the Kings of Judah remained lost until 1977, when they were unearthed during the construction of a parking lot. They'd been removed by rebel mobs, who thought the statues to be those of French kings. The originals are now on display in the **National Museum of the Middle Ages (5)** *(see also page 113).* Noted for its flying buttresses, gargoyles (you can climb up 387 steps in the North Tower to the **Galerie des Chimères** to view these famous

carved creatures), and two rose windows of stained glass, the cathedral is a marvel inside and out. Masterpieces of statuary cover the three main doors. Inside, statues, reliefs, paintings, and carved woodwork add to the grandeur. Kings and emperors were crowned beneath these lofty vaults.

Arts & Entertainment:

Notre-Dame (64), **Sainte-Chapelle (60)**, the **Conciergerie (61)**, and the **Crypte Archéologique (63)** are among Paris's most fascinating and oldest treasures. The stark and moving **Memorial of the Deportation (65)** *(Sq. de l'Île de France, 7 quai de l'Archevêché, 4th, at the eastern tip of Île de la Cité, 01-46.33.87.56, www.defense.gouv.fr.; hours: Oct–Mar Tu–Su 10AM–12PM, 2PM–5PM, Apr–Sep Tu–Su 10AM–12PM, 2PM–7PM)* is dedicated to the more than 200,000 French men, women, and children who died in WWII concentration camps.

PLACES TO EAT & DRINK
Where to Eat:

Restaurants aren't abundant in this area, so you might be better off eating on Île St-Louis. However, **Quai-Quai (66)** **(€€)** *(74 Quai des Orfevres, 1st, 01-46.33.69.75, http://quai-quai-restaurant.com; hours: Tu–Sa 12PM–2:30PM, 7:30PM–11PM)*, a classic bistro, serves good traditional French cuisine.

WHERE TO SHOP

The shopping here is basically limited to souvenirs and postcards. Stick to sightseeing and leave shopping for your spin around St-Germain.

WHERE TO STAY

There's not much in the way of lodging in this administrative district. Try Île St-Louis or other nearby areas (Marais, Latin Quarter, and St-Germain).

7 *to Pont Marie;* **10** *to Cardinal Lemoine*

• SNAPSHOT •

One of the most beautiful areas of Paris, the Île St-Louis is a haven of serenity and elegance between the bustle and noise of the Left and Right banks. Splendid 17th-century residences line calm streets, and along the romantic quays of the river the views are fabulous. It's a favorite residential area of artists and heiresses—and home to members of the Rothschild family. This is the perfect place to find a moment of repose after days of sightseeing.

PLACES TO SEE
Landmarks:

Stroll the periphery of the island: you'll find not only marvelous views of the city, but also lovely corners, beautiful residences, exquisite wrought-iron balconies, graceful doorways, and superb statuary. Check out the gargoyles that hold up the balcony at **Hôtel Chenizot (67)** *(51 rue St-Louis-en-l'Ile, 4th; closed to public)* and don't miss **Hôtel Lambert (68)** *(rue St-Louis-en-l'Ile at Quai d'Anjou, 4th; closed to public)*, a famous aristocratic 17th-century townhouse. The carved doors of the island church, **St-Louis-en-l'Ile (69)** *(19 bis, rue St-Louis-en-l'Ile, 4th, 01-46.34.11.60, www.saintlouisenlile.catholique.fr; hours: M–Sa 9:30AM–1PM, 2PM–7:30PM, Su 9AM–1PM, 2PM–7PM)*, are splendid; its clock and tower are also beautiful.

PLACES TO EAT & DRINK
Where to Eat:

With a spectacular view of Notre-Dame and the river, **Le Flore en l'Ile (70)** *(€€–€€€)* *(42 quai d'Orléans, 4th, 01-43.29.88.27, www.lefloreenlile.com; hours: daily 7AM–2AM)* is fabulous for breakfast, tea, desserts; less so for meals. Enjoy a great Alsatian meal at **Brasserie de l'Ile St-Louis (71)** *(€€)* *(55 quai de Bourbon, 4th, 01-43.54.02.59, www.labrasserie-isl.fr; hours: Th–Tu 12PM–11PM)*, a favorite of the island's cognoscenti. **Rue St-Louis-en-l'Ile** is the main drag with several appetizing eateries. For a light meal of quiche, salad, *crêpe*, and the like, **Au Lys d'Argent (72)** *(€)* *(90 rue St-Louis-en-l'Ile, 4th, 01-46.33.56.13, www.creperie-paris-ilesaintlouis.fr; hours: M, Th 12PM–10PM, Tu 12PM–3:30PM, F–Sa 12PM–10:30PM, Su 11:30AM–10PM)* satisfies many tastes and serves brunch daily. The chef at **Mon Vieil Ami (73)** *(€€)* *(69 rue St-Louis-en-l'Ile, 4th, 01-40.46.01.35, www.mon-vieil-ami.com; hours: W–Su 12PM–2PM, 6:30PM–11PM, closed 3 wks Jan & Aug)* creates imaginative, masterful Alsatian concoctions, lighter than the traditional modern fare, in a beautiful modern interior. For ethnic variety, **Sorza (74)** *(€€–€€€)* *(51 rue St-Louis-en-l'Ile, 4th, 01-43.54.78.62; hours: M–Sa 12PM–2:30PM, 6:30PM–10:30PM)* serves wonderful Italian dishes; tiny and sometimes cramped, it's romantically cozy outside rush hours. For a refreshing change, try **Isami (75)** *(€€)* *(4 quai d'Orléans, 4th, 01-*

PATISSERIE

40.46.06.97; *hours: Tu–Sa 12PM–2PM, 8PM–10PM)* for sushi and Japanese cuisine. Farm food and partying go hand-in-hand at **Nos Ancêtres les Gaulois (76)** (€€) *(39 rue St-Louis-en-l'Ile, 4th, 01-46.33.66.07, www.nos ancetreslesgaulois.com; hours: daily 7PM–2AM)*, an all-you-can-eat country inn with long trestle tables. A visit to Paris isn't complete without a stop at the famous ice cream parlor **Berthillon (77)** (€) *(31 rue St-Louis-en-l'Ile, 4th, 01-43.54.31.61, www.berthillon.fr; hours: W–Su 10AM–8PM, closed mid Jul–early Sep)*: all Parisians know it's the best around. Pastries, chocolates, pure fruit lollipops—**La Charlotte de l'Isle (78)** (€) *(24 rue St-Louis-en-l'Ile, 4th, 01-43.54.25.83, www.lacharlottedelisle.fr; hours: W–Su 11AM–7PM)* is a sweets lover's delight. The sign in the window says: "Here we sell happiness."

WHERE TO SHOP

Besides restaurants, **rue St-Louis-en-l'Ile** is also the main shopping street. The funny neckties and suspenders you may have seen at the Pompidou Center are made and sold at **Pylones (79)** *(57 rue St-Louis-en-l'Ile, 4th, 01-46.34.05.02, www.pylones.com; hours: daily 10:30AM–7:30PM)*. Stop in **Yamina (80)** *(56 rue St-Louis-en-l'Ile, 4th, 01-43.29.33.93; hours: M–Sa 10:30AM–1PM, 2PM–7:30PM, Su 2PM–7:30PM)* for hand-painted scarves and women's clothing. Beads galore, cords, and clasps—make your own jewelry masterpieces at **Le Grain de Sable (81)** *(79 rue St-Louis-en-l'Ile, 4th, 01-46.33.67.27, legraindesable.fr; hours: W–M 11AM–7PM, Tu 3PM–7PM)* or buy the salespeople's creations; hats are actually the centerpiece of this shop.

ST-GERMAIN
RUE DU BAC
MONTPARNASSE

Places to See:

Places to Eat & Drink:

★ *Top Picks*

Where to Shop:

Where to Stay:

ST-GERMAIN

④ to St-Germain-des-Prés, St-Sulpice,
St-Michel, or St-Placide;
⑩ to Mabillon; ④ ⑩ to Odéon;
⑫ to Rennes or Notre-Dame-des-Champs

● SNAPSHOT ●

St-Germain was once the stomping ground of artists, writers, and intellectuals and the locus of café society. Café life, always important in Paris, has been vital in St-Germain. Verlaine and Rimbaud drank themselves into poetic exaltation here. At the Café de Flore and Les Deux Magots, Sartre, de Beauvoir, and Camus developed their existentialist philosophies, often over coffee and endless cigarettes. Today, St-Germain remains the hub of the French publishing industry, but the writers and artists of the neighborhood are very well heeled. The elegant streets have been taken over by cutting-edge interior design showrooms and art galleries. High-profile fashion designers dot the landscape with their chic, artistic boutiques, making the district one of the finest for shopping. The upscale hip and cultural sophisticates mix with artists and intellectuals in this quarter where literati meet glitterati.

PLACES TO SEE
Landmarks:

The quarter takes its name from the medieval abbey around which it rose: **St-Germain-des-Prés (1)** *(3 pl. St-Germain-des-Prés, 6th, 01-55.42.81.10, www.eglise-sgp.org; hours: M–Sa 8AM–7:45PM, Su 9AM–8PM)* is the oldest church in Paris, dating from 542; it became a Benedictine abbey in the 8th century. It was rebuilt and restored over the centuries; the present church dates from the 11th century. Outside, a Picasso sculpture, **Hommage to Apollinaire (2)** *(rue de l'Abbaye & pl. St-Germain-des-Prés, 6th)*, was created in dedication to the artist's friend, poet Guillaume Apollinaire. One of Paris's most romantic spots is the tiny square **Place de Furstenberg (3)**, a favorite film location. There, the home of 19th-century Romantic painter Eugène Delacroix is now the **Delacroix Museum (4)** *(6 rue de Furstenberg, 6th, 01-44.41.86.50, www.musee-delacroix.fr; hours: W–M 9:30AM–5PM)*.

A result of Baron Haussmann's 19th-century urban planning, the wide, majestic **Blvd. St-Germain** is the main thoroughfare of the district. Replete with café terraces, restaurants, designer boutiques, and bookstores, the segment around the square of St-Germain is prime acreage for celebrity spottings. Some may be having a drink at one of the three most famous café-bars, noted for the writers, musicians, painters, and intellectuals who were regulars. In the 1920s and 1930s Hemingway, the Lost

Generation, and the surrealists, followed in the 1950s by existentialists, had their tables at **Les Deux Magots (5)** *(6 pl. St-Germain-des-Prés, 6th, 01-45.48.55.25, www.les deuxmagots.com; hours: daily 7:30AM–1AM)*. Poet Apollinaire held court at **Café de Flore (6)** *(172 bd. St-Germain, 6th, 01-45.48.55.26, www.cafedeflore.fr; hours: daily 7AM–2AM)*, claimed also by Sartre, Camus, and Simone de Beauvoir. Now the haunt of politicians and fashion designers, **Brasserie Lipp (7)** *(151 bd. St-Germain, 6th, 01-45.48.53.91, www.groupe-bertrand. com/lipp.php; hours: daily 9AM–1AM)* was once the meeting place for literary luminaries, such as Verlaine, Proust, Gide, and Malraux. Hemingway wrote *A Farewell to Arms* in this café; it has since been classified a historical monument. The next street westward, picturesque **rue du Dragon (8)** *(6th)*, dates from the Middle Ages, and still has 17th- and 18th-century houses.

Explore the narrow streets of the quarter, full of eye-catching boutiques and art galleries, as you make your way southward to splendid **Place St-Sulpice**, dominated by the Fountain of the Four Bishops and pink-flowered chestnut trees. Another popular movie location is **Café de la Mairie**. Construction of the church of **St-Sulpice (9)** *(pl. St-Sulpice, 6th, 01-42.34.59.98, 01-46.33.21.78, www.paroisse-saint-sulpice-paris.org & www. stsulpice.com; hours: daily 7:30AM–7:30PM)* took more than 100 years and is the result of the work of various architects.

The ★JARDIN DU LUXEMBOURG (10) *(60 acres encircled by bd. St-Michel, rue de Médicis, rue de Vaugirard, rue Guynemer, and rue August-Comte, 6th, www.senat.fr/visite/ jardin; hours: times vary; generally, summer daily 7:30AM–dusk, winter daily 8:15AM–dusk)* is Paris's most popular park. Formal terraces and wide walkways are adorned with statues of French queens. An octagonal pool, open-air café, puppet theater, bandstand, and tennis courts are also among the features of this splendid park. The gardens sweep down from the Florentine-style royal palace Palais du Luxembourg (11) *(15 rue de Vaugirard, 6th, 01-42.34.20.00, www.senat.fr; call to arrange visits)*, now seat of the French Senate. Like the palace, the imposing 17th-century Baroque Fontaine de Médicis (12) *(15 rue de Vaugirard, 6th)*, to the east, was built for Marie de Médici, Florentine widow of Henri IV.

Take rue de Vaugirard east to Théâtre National de l'Odéon (13) *(1 pl. Paul-Claudel, 6th, 01-44.85.40.40, www. theatre-odeon.fr; call for show times)*, once the home of classical theater company La Comédie Française. To the north, **rue de l'Odéon**, lined with 18th-century houses and shops, is where, at No. 12, Sylvia Beach opened the original Shakespeare & Co. bookshop *(see also page 112)*. Beach was a patron of writers such as F. Scott Fitzgerald and Ernest Hemingway. Largely thanks to her, James Joyce's *Ulysses* was first published in English. At the northern end of rue de l'Odéon, on Blvd. St-Germain, is the

TOP PICK!

Carréfour de l'Odéon, a square full of cinemas and student cafés—including Starbucks "de Paree"!

Cross Blvd. St-Germain and a few doors in on **rue de l'Ancienne-Comédie** is Le Procope (14) *(13 rue de l'Ancienne-Comédie, 6th, 01-40.46.79.00, www.procope. com; hours: Su–W 11:30AM–12AM, Th–Sa 11:30AM– 1AM)*, the world's first café, established in 1686. Voltaire was said to drink 40 cups of coffee there every day; Napoleon was another frequent customer. In the next street over, **Cour du Commerce St-André**, at No. 9, Dr. Guillotin developed his "philanthropic decapitating machine." Around the corner is the charming and quaint 15th-century series of courtyards, **Cour de Rohan (15)** *(access from rue du Jardinet & bd. St-Germain, 6th)*. The middle one has the only mounting block left in Paris, a *pas-de-mule* from which ladies and portly gentlemen mounted their mules.

Take rue Mazarine all the way to the Seine and the **Institut de France (16)** *(23 quai de Conti, 6th, 01-44.41.44.41, www.institut-de-france.fr; hours: closed to public, guided tours by appt, 2nd Su of each month)*, its majestic dome visible from afar. Home to five prestigious academies, the institute's most famous group of scholars is the Académie Française, entrusted since 1635 with publishing the definitive French dictionary. Going west along the river, you reach the famous **School of Fine Arts (Beaux-Arts) (17)** *(13 quai Malaquais, 6th, 01-47.03.50.00, www.ensba.fr; hours: Tu–Su 1PM–7PM)*, where artists and architects the world over have been trained.

Arts & Entertainment:

Guided tours of the **School of Fine Arts (Beaux-Arts) (17)** *(see previous page; school entrance 14 rue Bonaparte, 6th)* are by appointment only but the exhibition halls and bookstore are open to the public. The **Delacroix Museum (4)** *(see also page 137)* exhibits the painter's passionate canvases in his apartment and garden studio. The architectural mix of the abbey of **St-Germain-des-Prés (1)** *(see also page 137)* is noteworthy: 6th-century marble columns with Romanesque arches beneath Gothic vaults. A surviving original tower houses one of France's oldest belfries. The 17th-century philosopher René Descartes, among other notables, is buried here. If only in size, **St-Sulpice (9)** *(www.stsulpice.com, see also pages 138-139)* would be very impressive; the work of 20 artists makes it unique. In the chapel right of the entrance are three fabulous murals by Delacroix. St-Germain-des-Prés and St-Sulpice also regularly hold concerts.

The **Théâtre du Vieux Colombier (18)** *(21 rue du Vieux-Colombier, 6th, 01-44.39.87.00, vieux.colombier.free.fr; call for showtimes and bookings)* one of the venues of the Comédie Française *(see also page 52)*, presents French classics, notably the plays of Molière. The **Théâtre National de l'Odéon (13)** *(see also page 139)* specializes in foreign plays, in their original language. The work of Russian-born sculptor Ossip Zadkine is on display at the **Zadkine Museum (19)** *(100 bis, rue d'Assas, 6th, 01-55.42.77.20, www.zadkine.paris.fr; hours: Tu–Su 10AM–6PM)*, where the artist lived and worked for nearly 40 years. The works cover his artistic development, from Cubism to Expressionism and Abstractionism.

PLACES TO EAT & DRINK
Where to Eat:

St-Germain has so many good restaurants it's best to leave the three literary landmark cafés, Les Deux Magots (5), Café de Flore (6), and Brasserie Lipp (7) *(see page 138)*, for drinks and people watching. For cheap and retro, 1901 bistro **Le Petit St-Benoît (20)** (€) *(4 rue St-Benoît, 6th, 01-42.60.27.92, www.petit-st-benoit.com; hours: Tu–Sa 12PM–2:30PM, 7PM–10:30PM, closed Aug)* is a hoot; Marguerite Duras used to eat at the outdoor tables. Near the Beaux-Arts school and surrounded by galleries, **La Palette (21)** (€) *(43 rue de Seine, 6th, 01-43.26.68.15, www.cafelapaletteparis.com; hours: M–Sa 9AM–2AM, closed Aug)* is a neighborhood café full of students, art dealers, and artists. Great fish, wine, and Mediterranean food are part of the appeal of **Fish La Boissonnerie (22)** (€-€€) *(69 rue de Seine, 6th, 01-43.54.34.69; hours: M–Sa 12PM–2:30PM, 6:30PM–10:45PM)*. A best buy is **Cosi (23)** (€) *(54 rue de Seine, 6th, 01-46.33.35.36; hours: daily 12PM–11PM)*, a fabulous sandwich shop (it's not part of a chain). Japanese teppanyaki specialties, cooked in front of you, are exceptional at **Azabu (24)** (€€) *(3 rue André-Mazet, 6th, 01-46.33.72.05, azabu.fr; hours: Tu–Su 12:15PM–2PM, 7:15PM–10:15PM)*. The ghosts of Voltaire, Diderot, and Robespierre peer over your shoulder at Paris's oldest café-restaurant, Le Procope (14) (€-€€€) *(see also page 140)*.

Spit-roasted meats are the specialty at **La Rotisserie d'en Face (25)** (€€) *(2 rue Christine, 6th, 01-43.26.40.98, www.larotisseriecagna.fr; hours: M–Th 12PM–2:30PM,*

7PM–11PM, F 12PM–2:30PM, 7PM–11:30PM, Sa 7PM–11:30PM), frequented by businessmen and the chic alike. Eclectic food, snazzy minimalist décor, and an open, glass-paneled kitchen make **Ze Kitchen Galerie (26)** (€€€-€€€€) (4 rue des Grands-Augustins, 6th, 01-44.32.00.32, www.zekitchengalerie.fr; hours: M–F 12PM–2:30PM, 7PM–11PM, Sa 7PM–11PM) an artistic experience. For afternoon tea or weekend brunch, try **Mariage Frères (27)** (€-€€) (13 rue des Grands-Augustins, 6th, 01-40.51.82.50, www.mariagefreres.com; hours: daily 12PM–7PM, tea emporium & museum daily 10:30AM–7:30PM).

South of Blvd. St-Germain, a timeless bistro with delicious, simple, classic French food is **Aux Charpentiers (28)** (€€) (10 rue Mabillon, 6th, 01-43.26.30.05, www.aux charpentiers.fr; hours: daily 12PM–3PM, 7PM–11:30PM); it's authentic in both food and décor. Go for haute French at **Hélène Darroze (29)** (€€€-€€€€) (4 rue d'Assas, 6th, 01-42.22.00.11, www.helenedarroze.com, hours: lunch Tu–Sa 12:30PM–2:30PM, dinner Tu–Sa 7:30PM–10:30PM, reservations a must) or dine more casually in its downstairs **Salon d'Hélène** (€€-€€€). Delightful picnic food and scrumptious pastries make up for the window-counter seating at bakery **Gérard Mulot (30)** (€) (76 rue de Seine, 6th, 01-43.26.85.77, www.gerard-mulot.com; hours: Th–Tu 6:45AM–8PM, closed 4 wks Jul–Aug).

Experience a 1930s bistro lunch at **Le Comptoir du Relais (31)** (€€) (9 Carrefour de l'Odéon, 6th, 01-44.27.07.97, www.hotel-paris-relais-saint-germain.com; hours: daily 12PM–3PM, 8PM–11PM): it's small, has the requisite mirrored walls, and serves great grilled tuna, lamb, and rich cheeses. **Marco Polo (32) (€–€€)** *(8 rue de Condé, 6th, 01-43.26.79.63, www.restaurantmarco polo.fr; hours: daily 12PM–11PM)* is a popular Italian eatery. Delicious, not-to-be-missed: that's what they say about **Monsieur Le Prince (33) (€€)** *(12 rue Monsieur-le-Prince, 6th, 01-43.54.74.59; hours: Tu–Sa 12PM–2:30PM, 7PM–10:30PM, closed some days in Jul–Aug)*, a refined bistro.

Near Luxembourg Gardens, **La Bastide Odéon (34) (€–€€)** *(7 rue Corneille, 6th, 01-43.26.03.65, bastideodeon. com; hours: daily 12PM–2PM, 7PM–10:30PM)* offers memorable Provençal cooking in a cheerful setting. The simple country décor of **La Cuisine de Philippe (35) (€€)** *(25 rue Servandoni, 6th, 01-43.29.76.37; hours: Tu–Sa 12PM–2:15PM, 7PM–10:15PM)* complements its signature dish: the soufflé, both savory and sweet. Other traditional fare is also on the menu. The warmth of this small restaurant in a quiet street of an otherwise bustling neighborhood makes it a welcome retreat. At gem **Le Carré de Marguerite (36) (€–€€)** *(87 rue d'Assas, 6th, 01-43.26.33.61, www.lecarredemarguerite.fr; hours: Tu–F 12PM–2:30PM, 7:30PM–10:30PM, Sa 7:30PM–10:30PM)*, chef Gilles Choukroun is fabulous-ly innovative with nouvelle and North African cuisine. The Afro-Cuban music is great. For that very special night out, indulge in **Le Restaurant (37) (€€€€)** *(13 rue des Beaux-Arts, 6th, 01-44.41.99.01, www.l-hotel.com; hours: breakfast daily 7AM–10:30AM, lunch Tu–Sa 12:30PM–2:30PM, dinner Tu–Sa 7:30PM–10PM)*, located in **L'Hotel (66)**; modern French cuisine is served in opulent surrounds.

Bars & Nightlife:

A young crowd gathers at Canadian sports bar and grill **The Moose (38)** *(16 rue des Quatre-Vents, 6th, 01-46.33.77.00, www.mooseparis.com, hours: daily 11AM–12AM, lunch daily, brunch Su)*; it airs sports events and U.S. TV shows. Wine bar **La Crémerie Caves Miard (39)** *(9 rue des Quatre-Vents, 6th, 01-43.54.99.30, lacremerie.fr; hours: M–Sa 10:30AM–10PM, closed Aug)*, formerly a dairy shop, is adorably tiny, with a unique selection of wines. Friendly **Bob Cool Bar (40)** *(15 rue Grands Augustins, 6th, 01-46.33.33.77; hours: M–Sa 6PM–2AM, Su 6PM–12AM)* is a favorite with locals and visitors alike.

WHERE TO SHOP

From "hiply" conservative to avant-garde, St-Germain offers some of the best shopping in Paris. Style is the byword here, from clothes to art, furniture, and books. Antique shops, galleries, and eclectic interior designers abound in **rue Mazarine**, **rue Jacob**, **rue de Seine**, **rue Bonaparte**, and **rue des Saint-Pères**. The French design furniture at Alexandre Biaggi (41) *(14 rue de Seine, 6th, 01-44.07.34.73, www.alexandrebiaggi.com; hours: Tu–Sa 11AM–1PM, 2PM–7PM)* covers all the great names from the 1930s to 1950s. Clothing at Loft Design by (42) *(56 rue de Rennes, 6th, 01-45.44.88.99, www.loft designby.com)* is fashionably black or gray. The picturesque **open-air food market** at rue de Buci (43) *(on rue de Seine & rue de Buci, from bd. St-Germain, 6th, daily except Mondays)* finds Parisians engaged in a favorite pastime.

Discover exceptional furniture and sculpture from the 1940s to the 1970s at Galerie Yves Gastou (44) *(12 rue Bonaparte, 6th, 01-53.73.00.10, www.galerieyvesgastou. com)*. La Maison Ivre (45) *(38 rue Jacob, 6th, 01-42.60.01.85, www.maison-ivre.com; hours: M–Sa 10:30AM–7PM)* stocks ceramics and linens from Provence. Unusual antiques at Yveline (46) *(4 rue Furstenberg, 6th, 01-43.26.56.91, www.yveline-antiquites.com; hours: M–Sa 11AM–6:30PM)* delight even the most experienced shopper. The famous bookstore La Hune (47) *(16-18 rue de l'Abbaye, 6th, 01-45.48.35.85; hours: M–Sa 10AM–11:45PM, Su 11AM–7:45PM)* is known for its art, design, photography, and architecture books (in English and French), while its collection of fiction and critical works can keep you browsing 'til closing time.

Besides its beauty, **Blvd. St-Germain** is lined with great shops. Façonnable (48) *(174 bd. St-Germain, 6th, 01-40.49.02.47, www.faconnable.com)*, preppie with a French flair, is mostly men's wear but has a line for women. Parisian chic means comfortable skinny knits for women and casual elegance for men at Sonia Rykiel (49) *(175 bd. St-Germain, 6th, 01-49.54.60.60, www.soniarykiel.fr)*. Rykiel Enfant (50) *(4 rue de Grenelle, 6th, 01-49.54.61.10)* is the designer's line of children's fashions. For the Rykiel look that won't break the bank, head for **Sonia by Sonia Rykiel** *(6 rue de Grenelle, 6th, 01-49.54.61.00)*.

Lovely narrow streets south of Blvd. St-Germain, such as **rue du Four, rue de Rennes, rue Bonaparte, rue du Vieux-Colombier**—reveal a cornucopia of delights. Pastry chef extraordinaire Pierre Hermé (51) (72 rue Bonaparte, 6th, 01-43.54.47.77, www.pierreherme.com; hours: Su–W 10AM–7PM, Th–F 10AM–7:30PM, Sa 10AM–8PM) treats his work like high-end fashion by creating seasonal "collections." Those in the know line up for them. The glamorous lingerie at Sabbia Rosa (52) (71-73 rue des Sts-Pères, 6th, 01-45.48.88.37; hours: M–Sa 10AM–7PM) is worthy of its French starlet clientele; items can be made to order. For fresh young looks in jewelry, shop Agatha (53) (45 rue Bonaparte, 6th, 01-46.33.20.00, www.agatha.fr; hours: M–Sa 10AM–7PM). Shops along rue du Cherche-Midi are especially inviting. Robert Clergerie (54) (5 rue du Cherche-Midi, 6th, 01-45.48.75.47, www.robert clergerie.com) offers beauty and comfort in super stylish daytime shoes. A few doors away Poilâne (55) (8 rue du Cherche-Midi, 6th, 01-45.48.42.59, www.poilane.com; hours: M–Sa 7:15AM–8:15PM) makes its famous bread, along with other bakery delights. On Sunday mornings (9AM–1PM) organic market Marché Biologique (56) (bd. Raspail between rue du Cherche-Midi & rue de Rennes, 6th; hours: organic market Su 9AM–1PM; regular market Tu, F 7AM–1:30PM) is full of beautiful and delicious produce and products.

Leather designs in vibrant colors are the signature at Peggy Huyn Kinh (57) (11 rue Coëtlogon, 6th, 01-42. 84.83.82, www.phk.fr; hours: M–Sa 11AM–7PM). Longchamp (58) (21 rue du Vieux-Colombier, 6th, 01-42.22.74.75, www.longchamp.com; hours: M–Sa 10AM–7PM) doesn't stop at great handbags; its luggage collection is just as wonderful. Vanessa Bruno (59) (25 rue St-Sulpice, 6th, 01-

43.54.41.04, www.vanessabruno.com) designs—flatter-ing, feminine, and sporty—are extremely popular. Chasing cool? You'll find it at Carven Boutique (60) *(36 rue St-Sulpice, 09-60.45.47.04, www.carven.fr; hours: M–Sa 10:30AM–7:30PM)*, known for contemporary upmarket fashion.

Master *chocolatier* Christian Constant (61) *(37 rue d'Assas, 6th, 01-53.63.15.15, www.christianconstant.com; hours: M–F 8:30AM–9PM, Sa–Su 8:30AM–8:30PM)* seeks inspi-ration around the globe for his creations. Way cool fash-ion for women and men at APC (62) *(38 rue Madame, 6th, 01-42.22.12.77, www.apc.fr; hours: M–Sa 11AM–7:30PM, Su 12:30PM–6:30PM)*, designed by Jean Touitou, has followers all over Paris *(past-season items are discounted at 45 rue Madame, 6th, 01-45.48.43.71).* Exceptional architecture and design books are the focus at Librairie le Moniteur (63) *(7 pl. de l'Odéon, 6th, 01-44.41.15.75, www.librairiedumoniteur.com; hours: Tu–Sa 10:30AM–7PM).* Is it sculpture? Or is it edible? Some claim Patrick Roger (64) *(91 rue de Rennes, 6th, 01-45.44.66.13, www.patrickroger.com; hours: M–Sa 10:30AM–7:30PM)* is the Rodin of ganache. His choco-late creations are not just beautiful to look at but are sublimely delicious. Le Mouton à Cinq Pattes (65) *(138 bd. St-Germain, 6th, 01-43.26.49.25, www.moutona cinqpattesparis.com; hours: M–Sa 10AM–7PM)* unearths vintage designer clothes and last season's numbers. The store has two other outlets *(8 & 18 rue Saint-Placide, 6th, 01-45.48.86.26 & 01-42.84.25.11).*

WHERE TO STAY

Famous 19th-century guests created delicious scandals at **L'Hôtel (66)** (€€€-€€€€) *(13 rue des Beaux-Arts, 6th, 01-44.41.99.00, www.l-hotel.com)*; Oscar Wilde died there and music-hall star Mistinguett was a regular. Still frequented by celebrities, the hotel is flamboyant and wonderful. Charming and well-managed, **Hôtel du Danube Saint-Germain (67)** (€€) *(58 rue Jacob, 6th, 01-42.60.34.70, www.hoteldanube.fr)* has spacious rooms in a mix of styles. A walled garden, wood-paneled rooms, and many small details make a stay at **Hôtel St-Germain-des-Prés (68)** (€€) *(36 rue Bonaparte, 6th, 01-43.26.00.19, www.hotel-paris-saint-germain.com)* special.

Romantic, small, and charming **Hôtel d'Angleterre (69)** (€€) *(44 rue Jacob, 6th, 01-42.60.34.72, www. hotel-angleterre-paris.net)* welcomes guests warmly. A 17th-century town house with beamed ceilings and Aubusson tapestries, **Hôtel d'Aubusson (70)** (€€€-€€€€) *(33 rue Dauphine, 6th, 01-43.29.43.43, www.hoteldaubusson. com)* is beautifully decorated.  Dignified but not stuffy, **Au Manoir St-Germain-des-Prés (71)** (€€-€€€) *(153 bd. St-Germain, 6th, 01-42.22.21.65, www.paris-hotels-charm.com)* is charming and comfortable, with large bedrooms and airy common rooms. The **Artus Hôtel (72)** (€€-€€€) *(34 rue de Buci, 6th, 01-43.29.07.20, www.artushotel.com)*, with its zebra-patterned armchairs, stone fountain, and doors hand-painted by local artists, is unusual, imaginative, and chic, with simple, well-designed rooms.

Oriental rugs, tapestries, brocades, and arbors of blooming plants enhance the thick beams and stone walls of **Grand Hôtel de l'Univers (73)** (€–€€) *(6 rue Grégoire-de-Tours, 6th, 01-43.29.37.00, www.hotel-paris-univers.com).* Beautiful **Le Madison Hôtel (74)** (€€€–€€€€) *(143 bd. St-Germain, 6th, 01-40.51.60.00, www.hotel-madison.com)*—its sitting areas adorned with tapestries and antiques—combines modern amenities in the rooms with conventional furnishings, evoking the gracious charm of old inns. A great location and cheap prices make up for the small, worn-out rooms in the clean, unpretentious **Welcome Hôtel (75)** (€) *(66 rue de Seine, 6th, 01-46.34.24.80, www.hotelwelcomeparis.com).*

Oak beams, stone walls, Aubusson tapestries, and an abundance of fresh flowers give **Hôtel Left Bank St-Germain (76)** (€–€€€) *(9 rue de l'Ancienne-Comédie, 6th, 01-43.54.01.70, www.paris-hotels-charm.com)* much of its allure; the standard-size rooms are comfortable. Gracious common areas in the appealing **Hôtel de Fleurie (77)** (€€–€€€) *(32 rue Grégoire-de-Tours, 6th, 01-53.73.70.00, www.hotel-de-fleurie.fr)* are matched by rooms with a good layout and marble bathrooms. Location is the advantage of **Atlantis St-Germain-des-Prés (78)** (€–€€) *(4 rue du Vieux-Colombier, 6th, 01-45.48.31.81, www.hotelatlantis-sg.com)*, across from St-Sulpice Church; clean rooms are decorated in a mix of Art Deco and traditional French. Nearby, at spectacular **Hôtel de l'Abbaye (79)** (€€€) *(10 rue Cassette, 6th, 01-45.44.38.11, www.hotelabbayeparis.com)*, once a 16th- and 17th-century convent, the cobblestone courtyard leads to a splendid reception and salon, while top-floor suites offer fireplaces, arched ceilings, and rooftop views. A super-cheap sleep across from the Luxembourg Gardens, **Pension Les Marronniers (80)** (€) *(78 rue d'Assas, 6th, 01-43.26.37.71, www.pension-marronniers.com)* is a fast-disappearing species, a pension with breakfast and dinner included; most bedrooms, basic and clean, share bathrooms.

RUE DU BAC

12 *to Solférino or rue du Bac;* **10** **12** *to Sèvres-Babylone*

• SNAPSHOT •

The rue du Bac, an area of high-end design and fashion, is a slice of the Left Bank snuggled between sophisticated, hip St-Germain and refined, aristocratic Invalides. Elegant residential facades give a more sedate air to the neighborhood, though boutiques and restaurants claim the cream of French architectural and interior design—with names such as Philippe Starck, Andrée Putman, and Christian Biecher. The spectacular Musée d'Orsay is one of the highlights in this quarter.

PLACES TO SEE
Landmarks:

The **Quai Voltaire** has great river views of Concorde, the Tuileries Gardens, and the Louvre. Famous residents of the street include: Louise de Kéroualle, spy for Louis XIV, at Nos. 3-5; composers Richard Wagner and Jean Sibelius, poet Charles Baudelaire, and writer-pundit Oscar Wilde at No. 19; while No. 27 is where philosopher Voltaire died. Further east is the superb ★MUSÉE D'ORSAY (81) *(1 rue de la Légion-d'Honneur at Quai Anatole France, 7th, 01-40.49.48.14, www.musee-orsay.fr; hours: Tu–Su 9:30AM–6PM, Th 9:30AM–9:45PM)*. Dedicated to artistic creation from 1848 to 1914, it includes works by Carpeaux, Cézanne, Daumier,

TOP PICK!

Degas, Delacroix, Gauguin, Manet, Monet, Renoir, Rodin, and van Gogh, among others. The collection of Impressionist art belonging to the Jeu de Paume before it closed in 1986 is now housed here. Once a train station, the building itself  is as magnificent as the art it houses. Retaining much of the original architecture and ironwork, the museum's interior is lofty, airy, and spacious, the openness enhanced by wide exhibition spaces on multiple levels.

Rue du Bac is a classy street lined with elegant boutiques. The buildings and storefronts, many designed by France's top interior decorators, are as fascinating to look at as the wares inside. At the southern end of rue du Bac, you come to **Le Bon Marché (82)** *(24 rue de Sèvres, 7th, 01-44.39.80.00, www.lebonmarche.fr; hours: M–W, Sa 10AM–8PM, Th–F 10AM–9PM)*, Paris's first department store. Designed by Gustave Eiffel, creator of the Eiffel Tower, the *fin-de-siècle* and Art Deco decoration of this landmark inspire some of the awe that Paris wins and deserves.

Arts & Entertainment:

The **Musée d'Orsay (81)** *(see also page 152)* houses a stunning collection of Impressionist paintings, Art Nouveau pieces, mid-to-late-19th-century works, and late-19th-century through early-20th-century paintings and sculptures. Architectural reproductions cover

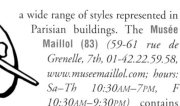

a wide range of styles represented in Parisian buildings. The **Musée Maillol (83)** *(59-61 rue de Grenelle, 7th, 01-42.22.59.58, www.museemaillol.com; hours: Sa–Th 10:30AM–7PM, F 10:30AM–9:30PM)* contains the artist's voluptuous sculptures and other works. It also includes works by Rodin, Picasso, and Cézanne, among others.

PLACES TO EAT & DRINK
Where to Eat:

For fabulous fresh breads, pastries, sandwiches, and more, stop by **Eric Kayser (84)** (€) *(18 rue du Bac, 7th, 01-42.61.27.63, www.maison-kayser.com; hours: Tu–Su 7AM–8PM)*. If jet-set bistro **Le Voltaire (85)** (€€-€€€) *(27 Quai Voltaire, 7th, 01-42.61.17.49; hours: M–Sa 12PM–2:30PM, 7:30PM–10PM, closed Aug)* makes your head spin, the affordable café next door, **Le Petit Voltaire**, serves delicious soups and omelettes. Museum eatery **Restaurant du Musée d'Orsay (86)** (€-€€) *(1 rue du Légion d'Honneur, 7th, 01-45.49.47.03, www.musee-orsay.fr; hours: Tu–Su 9:30AM–5:45PM, Th 9:30AM–2:45PM, 7PM–9PM)* offers lunch and tea in a spectacular setting with a magnificent view. For a light meal, the tearoom **Les Nuits des Thés (87)** (€) *(22 rue de Beaune, 7th, 01-47.03.92.07, www.lesnuitsdesthes.com; hours: M–Sa 11AM–7PM, Su 3:30PM–7PM)* is pleasant and relaxing. The old-fashioned refinement of the quarter's dignified upper crust is reflected in the décor and menu at **La Calèche (88)** (€€) *(8 rue de Lille, 7th, 01-42.60.24.76; hours: M–Sa 12:15PM–2:30PM, 7:15PM–10:30PM, closed 2 wks Aug)*.

Culinary hot spot **L'Atelier de Joël Robuchon (89)** (€€-€€€€) *(5 rue de Montalembert, 7th, 01-42.22.56.56, www.joel-robuchon.net; hours: daily 11:30AM–3:30PM, 6:30PM–12AM)* is a unique experience: you sit at U-shaped counters and taste tapas-like morsels of food for the gods. The souf-flés are exceptional at **La Cigale Récamier (90)** (€€-€€€) *(4 rue Récamier, 7th, 01-45.48.86.58; hours: M–Sa 12PM–2:30PM, 7PM–11PM)*. French standards prepared in large portions by the motherly owner of **Au Babylone (91)** (€) *(13 rue de Babylone, 7th, 01-45.48.72.13; hours: M–Sa 12:30PM–2:30PM, closed Aug)* satisfy anyone's nostalgia for typical French lunches of the past.

Audacious, light, clever, out of this world—these are some of the ways people describe the creations of chef-owner Claude Colliot at **Le Bamboche (92)** (€€-€€€) *(15 rue de Babylone, 7th, 01-45.49.14.40, www.le bamboche.com; hours: M–Sa 12PM–2:30PM, 7PM–11PM, Su 7PM–11PM, book ahead)*. The in-store restaurant at **Le Bon Marché (82)**, **Primo Piano (93)** (€€-€€€) *(Le Bon Marché, 1st floor, 26 rue de Sèvres, 7th, 01-42.22.02.42, www.lebonmarche.com; hours: M–Sa 11AM–6:30PM)*, designed by Leo Berellini, features a light Tuscan menu with fresh products in season. More budget-conscious choices at Le Bon Marché include **Le Café de la Grande Épicerie** and **Le Comptoir Picnic**.

Reserve in advance for **L'Epi Dupin (94)** (€€) *(11 rue Dupin, 6th, 01-42.22.64.56, www.epidupin.com; hours: M 7PM–11PM, Tu–F 12PM–3PM, 7PM–11PM, closed Aug)*, near the Bon Marché, serving refined bistro classics in a friendly atmosphere (it gets hectic at rush hours, but the consensus is it's worth it). Have coffee or lunch, relax, and watch the world go by at **La Frégate (95)** (€€) *(1 rue du Bac, 7th, 01-42.61.23.77, www.lafregateparis.com; hours: restaurant daily 11:30AM–11:30PM, cafe daily 7AM–1AM)*, across from the Seine and the Louvre. For a change of pace, try the restaurant in the Latin American cultural center **La Maison de l'Amérique Latine (96)** (€€–€€€) *(217 bd. St-Germain, 7th, 01-49.54.75.10, www.mal217.org; hours: Oct–Apr M–F lunch only, May–Sep M–F lunch & dinner, prix-fixe menus)*. The menu is an unusual combination of French and Argentinian cuisine; during summer, lunch is served in a splendid garden under white umbrellas.

Bars & Nightlife:

This quiet, refined quarter tends to close shop early. St-Germain is more conducive to nightlife.

WHERE TO SHOP

Browse the many *antiquaires* in this quarter. The shops of **Carré Rive Gauche (97)** *(16 rue des St-Pères, 7th, bordered by quai Voltaire, rue des St-Pères, rue de l'Université, & rue du Bac, www.carrerivegauche.com)*, an association of antique dealers, carry quality items from rustic to the grandiose. Adorable *fromagerie* **Barthélémy (98)** *(51 rue de*

Grenelle, 7th, 01-42.22.82.24, 01-45.48.56.75; hours: Tu–F 8:30AM–1PM, 4PM–7:30PM, Sa 8:30AM–1:30PM, 3PM–7PM) is a must for cheese lovers. Marvelous Magna Carta (99) (101 rue du Bac, 7th, 01-45.48.02.49, www.magna-carta.fr; hours: M–Sa 11AM–7PM) stocks trendy gifts and paper goods. The chocolates magnificently displayed at Debauve & Gallais (100) (30 rue des Sts-Pères, 7th, 01-45.48.54.67, www.debauve-et-gallais.fr; hours: M–Sa 9AM–7PM) are among the most divine; you can order online from abroad. Alain Mikli (101) (74 rue des Sts-Pères, 7th, 01-45.49.40.00, www.mikli.fr; hours: M–Sa 10AM–7PM) carries the designer's signature eyeglasses as well as his funky, futuristic ready-to-wear collection and handbags. Exquisite chocolates at Richart (102) (258 bd. St-Germain, 7th, 01-45.55.66.00, www.richart.com; hours: M–Sa 10AM–7PM) come with tips on chocolate appreciation. You'll find a colorful array of accessories, including umbrellas, scarves, socks, and more at Gérard Durand (103) (75-77 rue du Bac, 7th, 01-45.44.98.55, www.accessoires-mode.com; hours: M–Sa 9AM–7PM). Nine perfume makers have created the unique scents at Editions de Parfums Frédéric Malle (104) (37 rue de Grenelle, 7th, 01-42.22.76.40, www.fredericmalle.com; hours: M 12PM–7PM, Tu–Sa 11PM–7PM).

Famous French interior designer Christian Liaigre (105) (42 rue du Bac, 7th, 01-53.63.33.66, www.christian-liaigre.fr) has decorated hotels, stores, and restaurants in Paris and New York; his furniture and lighting creations are sold here. For four generations Ryst-Dupeyron (106) (79 rue du Bac, 7th, 01-45.48.80.93, 09-54.39.72.78, *www.ryst-dupeyron.com; hours: M–F 9:30AM–6PM)* has sold *armagnac* and fine spirits; its bottled treasures date from 1868.

Le Bon Marché (82) *(see also page 153)* offers the latest fashions for both women and men, as well as its own (less expensive) brand. The food hall, La Grande Épicerie, presents luscious displays in a grand setting.

WHERE TO STAY

If your priority is peace and quiet, this sedate neighborhood might be just the thing. Understated, tasteful rooms at **Hôtel d'Orsay (107)** *(€€-€€€) (93 rue de Lille, 7th, 01-47.05.85.54, www.paris-hotel-orsay.com, www.esprit-de-france.com)* are warmly decorated and reasonably priced. Clean and quiet, **Hôtel Bersoly's St-Germain (108)** *(€€) (28 rue de Lille, 7th, 01-42.60.73.79, www.bersolyshotel.com)* offers basic amenities. In a 17th-century building with original cross beams and stone walls, the small, charming **Hôtel Verneuil (109)** *(€€-€€€) (8 rue de Verneuil, 7th, 01-42.60.82.14, www.hotel-verneuil-saint-germain.com)* is run by an art collector who has made it her mission to make you feel like a guest in her home.

The renovated **Hôtel de l'Université (110)** *(€-€€€) (22 rue de l'Université, 7th, 01-42.61.09.39, www.universite*

hotel.com) offers large, comfortable, light-filled rooms. Some are modern; others have rafters and wainscoting. You'll enjoy breakfast in the lounge enclosed by stained glass windows. An arty crowd appreciates the Art Deco lobby with its elephant and panther statues, as well as the jazz bar at **Hôtel Lenox St-Germain (111)** (€-€€€) *(9 rue de l'Université, 7th, 01-42.96.10.95, www.hotel-parislenoxsaintgermain.com)*; rooms are more classically furnished.

Rooms at the elegant **Le Montalembert (112)** (€€€-€€€€) *(3 rue Montalembert, 7th, 01-45.49.68.68, www. hotel-montalembert.fr)* vary enormously in style, from contemporary chic to Louis-Philippe pomp. Simple, smart, and well-designed, **Hôtel St. Thomas d'Aquin (113)** (€€) *(3 rue Pré-aux-Clercs, 7th, 01-42.61.01.22, www. hotel-st-thomas-daquin.com)* is an excellent deal; therefore, usually booked.

Sumptuous and distinguished, the luxurious Regency-styled **Hôtel Duc de Saint-Simon (114)** (€€-€€€) *(14 rue de St-Simon, 7th, 01-44.39.20.20, www.hotelducdesaint simon.com)* caters to a discerning clientele. At the grand Left Bank establishment **Hôtel Lutétia (115)** (€€-€€€€) *(45 bd. Raspail, 6th, 01-49.54.46.46, toll-free from U.S. & Canada 1-800-888-4747, www.lutetia-paris.com),* the rooms are plush, the hallways graced with statues, and the service impeccable.

MONTPARNASSE

④ ⑥ ⑫ ⑬ *to Montparnasse-Bienvenüe;* ④ *to Vavin;*
⑥ *to Edgar Quinet;* ⑬ *to Gaîté;*
④ ⑥ *to Raspail or Denfert-Rochereau*

● SNAPSHOT ●

Montparnasse was once the neighborhood of illustrious artists: Picasso, Léger, Soutine, Braque, Modigliani, Chagall, Zadkine, and Man Ray lived there, as did writers Gertrude Stein, Henry Miller, and Ezra Pound. Between the two World Wars it was the symbol of moder-

nity, a hotbed of intellectual and artistic creativity. Those days are long gone. The first Parisian skyscraper, the Tour Montparnasse, caused horror in the 1970s, resulting in changes in building regulations. The area has unfortu-

nately suffered from tragic urban development policies, but it's worth a trip just to visit the haunts of some of the 20th century's great cultural and artistic figures.

PLACES TO SEE
Landmarks:

The Tour Montparnasse (116) *(33 ave. du Maine, 15th, 01-45.38.52.56, www.tourmontparnasse56.com; hours: Apr–Sep daily 9:30AM–11:30PM; Oct–Mar Su–Th 9:30AM–10:30PM, F–Sa 9:30AM–11PM)* was the biggest office building in Europe when it was built in 1973. An observation deck on the 56th floor provides good views of the city, as does the rooftop terrace. Below, the café-restaurant **La Coupole (117)** *(102 bd. du Montparnasse, 14th, 01-43.20.14.20, www.lacoupole-paris.com; hours: daily 8:30AM–12AM)* has had a famous artistic clientele, including Jean-Paul Sartre, Josephine Baker, and Roman Polanski. **La Closerie des Lilas (118)** *(171 bd. du Montparnasse, 6th, 01-40.51.34.50, www.closeriedes lilas.fr; hours: daily 12PM–1AM)* was the favorite café-bar of Hemingway, F. Scott Fitzgerald, Lenin, and Trotsky. The café is practically a character in Hemingway's novel *The Sun Also Rises*, which he wrote on the terrace in six weeks. Art Deco buildings ornament **rue Campagne-Première (119)** *(14th)*, the street where many artists lived between the two World Wars; among them Picasso, Kandinsky, and Joan Miró. Modigliani, suffering from tuberculosis and opium addiction, lived in No. 3.

The **Montparnasse Cemetery (120)** *(3 bd. Edgar-Quinet, 14th, 01-44.10.86.50; hours: Mar 16–Nov 5 M–F 8AM–6PM, Sa 8:30AM–6PM, Su 9AM–6PM; Nov 6–Mar 15 M–F 8AM–5:30PM, Sa 8:30AM–5:30PM, Su 9AM–5:30PM)*, commissioned by Napoleon, is the resting place of many famous writers and artists. Among them are: Samuel Beckett, Charles Baudelaire, Jean-Paul Sartre, Simone de Beauvoir, Guy de Maupassant, Tristan Tzara, Eugene Ionesco, Constantin Brancusi, Frédéric Bartholdi (sculptor of the Statue of Liberty), Man Ray, Chaïm Soutine, Jean Seberg, Camille Saint-Saëns, André Citroën, Serge Gainsbourg, and Henri Laurens.

Beneath the streets of Paris runs a 3,000-km network of tunnels (nearly 2,000 miles). Just before the French Revolution, the bones of six million Parisians were transferred by wheelbarrow from overcrowded city cemeteries to the **Catacombs (121)** *(1 ave. Colonel Henri-Rol-Tanguy, 14th, 01-43.22.47.63, www. catacombes-de-paris.fr; hours: Tu–Su 10AM–5PM, ticket office closes 4PM)*. During the Reign of Terror, more bodies were placed there. The bones of Marat, Robespierre, and other French citizens are packed in layer upon layer of skulls and bones, all on public display some 25 yards below the streets of the city.

Arts & Entertainment:

The **Musée du Montparnasse (122)** *(21 ave. du Maine, 15th, 01-42.22.91.96, www.museedumontparnasse.net; hours: Tu–Su 12:30PM–7PM)* captures the ethos of this early 20th century bohemian quarter in a former hang-out for artists such as Picasso, Modigliani, and Chagall. The **Fondation Henri Cartier-Bresson (123)** *(2 impasse Lebouis, 14th, 01-56.80.27.00, www.henricartierbresson. org; hours: W 1PM–8:30PM; Tu–F, Su 1PM–6:30PM; Sa 11AM–6:45PM)* is a museum dedicated to the works of the great French photographer. The **Fondation Cartier pour l'Art Contemporain (124)** *(261 bd. Raspail, 14th, 01-42.18.56.50, www.fondation.cartier.com; hours: Tu 11AM–10PM, W–Su 11AM–8PM)*, a center for contemporary art, theater, music, and dance, is housed in a spectacular glass building designed by Jean Nouvel.

PLACES TO EAT & DRINK
Where to Eat:

Montparnasse was a social hub for early 20th-century artists and writers. It was common to sight the likes of Picasso, Modigliani, Cocteau, Apollinaire, Hemingway, and F. Scott Fitzgerald along Boulevard du Montparnasse.  Imagine discussing feminism with Simone de Beauvoir over an *apéritif* at the Art Deco-styled **La Coupole (117)** *(€€–€€€) (102 bd. du Montparnasse, 14th, 01-43.20.14.20, www.lacoupole-paris.com; hours: Su–W 12PM–12AM, Th–Sa 12PM–1AM, breakfast M–F from 8AM, Sa–Su from 8:30AM)*. Today, one goes there because of its illustrious history, not for the food; drinks will do the trick just as well. On the other hand, **Le Dôme (125)** *(€€€) (108 bd. du Montparnasse, 14th, 01-43.35.25.81; hours: daily 12PM–3PM, 7PM–11:30PM, closed Su–M in Aug)*, that other Montparnasse institution, offers fabulous fish and seafood in a superb Art Deco interior.

In a street full of *crêperies*, don't miss **Crêperie de Josselin (126)** *(€) (67 rue du Montparnasse, 14th, 01-43.20.93.50; hours: Tu–Su 12PM–11PM)*; lovely, romantic, and as relaxed as the Breton countryside, the whole experience is most satisfying. Have a hankering for Italian? **Auberge de Venise (127)** *(€€) (10 rue Delambre, 14th, 01-43.35.43.09, www.aubergedevenise.fr; hours: daily 11:30AM–2:45PM, 6PM–11:45PM, closed Aug)* assures good food and a comfortable ambience.

In tiny bistro **Chez Marcel (128) (€€)** *(7 rue Stanislas, 6th, 01-45.48.29.94; hours: M–F 12PM–2PM, 7:30PM–10PM, closed Aug)* you feel like you're a guest in the chef's home: Lyonnais cuisine is matched by friendly service and unpretentious décor. Imaginative bistro fare and a great wine list put **Wadja (129) (€€)** *(10 rue de la Grande-Chaumière, 6th, 01-46.33.02.02; hours: M 7:30PM–11PM, Tu–Sa 12PM–2PM, 7:30PM–11PM)* on the "good value" list. **Caméléon (130) (€€–€€€)** *(6 rue de Chevreuse, 6th, 01-43.27.43.27, cameleonjeanpaularabianparis.com; hours: Tu–Sa 12PM–2:15PM, 7PM–10:45PM)* is an old-fashioned bistro—low-key with classic French food.

Bars & Nightlife:

Watch the world go by at the famous café-bars on **Blvd. du Montparnasse**: La Coupole (117) *(No. 102, see pages 161 & 163)*, Le Dôme (125) *(No. 108, see page 163)*, or **Le Select (131)** *(99 bd. du Montparnasse, 6th, 01-45.48.38.24; hours: M–F, 7AM–3AM, Sa–Su 7AM–4AM)*. The Fondation Cartier (124) *(see also page 162)* hosts very hip arts soirées. **Rosebud (132)** *(11 bis, rue Delambre, 14th, 01-43.35.38.54; hours: daily 7PM–2AM)*, a 1950s-style café-bar, attracts a chic, more mature (30ish to 50ish), arty and media crowd with its retro glamour.

WHERE TO SHOP

The **open-air food market** at rue Daguerre (133) *(between ave. du Maine & ave. du Général-Leclerc, 14th; hours: Tu–Su morning, late afternoon)* is a daily feast. But food isn't the only offering here: don't forget to check out the shops. For example you'll find adorable outfits for children, linens, lace, cosmetics, and food products made by nuns and monks throughout France at La Boutique de l'Artisanat Monastique (134) *(68 bis, ave. Denfert-Rochereau, 14th, 01-43.35.15.76, www.artisanat monastique.com; hours: M–F 12PM–6:30PM, Sa 2PM–7PM)*. The quality is superb.

WHERE TO STAY

An international clientele creates an appealing atmosphere at Hôtel Lenox Montparnasse (135) (€–€€) *(15 rue Delambre, 14th, 01-43.35.34.50, www.hotellenox.com)*, where personality makes up for room size. Surrealist André Breton once lived in the building now occupied by Hôtel Delambre (136) (€) *(35 rue Delambre, 14th, 01-43.20.66.31, www.delambre-paris-hotel.com)*, a comfortable, affordable sleep. More formal, Hôtel l'Aiglon (137) (€–€€) *(232 bd. Raspail, 14th, 01-43.20.82.42, www. paris-hotel-aiglon.com)* is discreet and tasteful. South of rue Daguerre, Hôtel Sophie Germain (138) (€) *(12 rue Sophie Germain,14th, south of our map border, check Web site for location, 01-43.21.43.75, www.hotelsophie germain.com)* is an excellent value for business or leisure travelers.

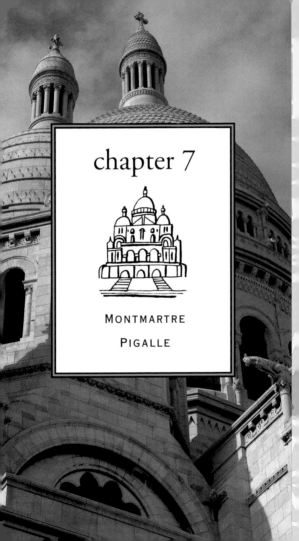

chapter 7

MONTMARTRE

PIGALLE

MONTMARTRE
PIGALLE

Places to See:

1. Place des Abbesses
2. St-Jean-de-Montmartre
3. Chapelle du Martyre
4. Square Willette
5. SACRÉ-COEUR ★
6. Place du Tertre
7. Au Lapin Agile
8. Moulin de la Galette
9. Avenue Junot
10. Le Bateau-Lavoir
11. Max Fourny Museum of Naïf Art
12. Espace Montmartre Salvador Dali
13. Musée de Montmartre
14. Studio 28
15. Théâtre de l'Atelier
34. Montmartre Cemetery
35. Moulin Rouge
36. Museum of Eroticism

Places to Eat & Drink:

16. L' Été en Pente Douce
17. Le Moulin de la Galette
18. Le Soleil Gourmand
19. Café Burq
20. La Famille
21. L'Annexe
22. L'Entracte
23. La Bascule
37. L'Homme Tranquille
38. Chez Toinette
39. Rose Bakery
40. Le Divan du Monde
41. La Fourmi

Where to Shop:

24. Pages 50/70: Olivier Verlet
25. Zelia sur la Terre comme au Ciel
26. Galerie Christine Diegoni
27. Belle de Jour
28. Marché St-Pierre
29. Luc Dognin
30. Lily Latifi
42. Et puis c'est tout
43. Emmanuelle Zysman
44. Patricia Louisor

★ *Top Pick*

As an artist, a man has no home
in Europe save in Paris.

—*Friedrich Nietzsche*

MONTMARTRE

 *to Abbesses or Lamarck-Caulaincourt*

• SNAPSHOT •

For centuries Montmartre was a serene village, full of windmills, thatched cottages, and vineyards. However, it gained its name by quite an un-serene history. It is the site of the beheading of St. Denis and other Christian priests by the Romans in A.D. 250. The *Mons Martyrum*, or Mound of the Martyrs, later evolved into Montmartre. The highest point in the city, it became part of Paris in 1860 but retained its village-like character, regardless of Baron Haussmann's renovations. From the 1880s artists began moving into the area, giving it the bohemian lifestyle and reputation for which it is still known today. Montmartre was the inspiration for works by Renoir, Toulouse-Lautrec, Utrillo, Modigliani, and Picasso, among others. Atop the hill the enormous basilica of Sacré-Coeur, with its pristine white dome, is visible from just about anywhere in Paris; from there the panorama of the city unfolds in all its glory. Today, Montmartre is again a quarter of emerging young artists and the next generation of fashion designers. It retains its village-like charm, and the romantic aura of the streets on the hill never seems to fade. Make sure to roam those streets to absorb the allure of the quarter and note its many beautiful details.

PLACES TO SEE
Landmarks:

Only two Métro stations still have their original Art Nouveau wrought iron and glass-canopied entrances

designed by Hector Guimard: Porte Dauphine, on Paris's western edge, and Abbesses, in the heart of Montmartre at **Place des Abbesses (1)** *(18th)*, a lively, picturesque square. **St-Jean-de-Montmartre (2)** *(19 rue des Abbesses, 18th, 01-46.06.43.96, www.saintjeandemontmartre.com; hours: M–Sa 9AM–7PM, Su 9:30AM–6PM)*, the first church to be built of reinforced concrete, is faced with brick; its door is inlaid with turquoise mosaics, and the interior is Art Nouveau with details borrowed from Islamic architecture. Legend has it that when St. Denis, the first bishop of Paris, was decapitated in a medieval chapel, he picked up his head and walked away. Today, the **Chapelle du Martyre (3)** *(9 rue Yvonne-le-Tac, 18th; hours: chapel Tu–Su 10AM–6PM; crypt F 3PM–6PM)* stands on that site.

TOP PICK!

A short walk along rue Tardieu brings you to **Square Willette (4)** *(18th)*. With lawns, trees, shrubs, and flowerbeds terraced into its hillside setting, ★**SACRÉ-COEUR (5)** *(35 rue du Chevalier de la Barre, 18th, 01-53.41.89.00, www.sacre-coeur-montmartre.com; hours: daily 6AM–10:30PM; dome hours: summer daily 9AM–7PM, winter* *daily 9AM–6PM*), the **Basilica of the Sacred Heart**, is a grand Roman-Byzantine church. During the Franco-Prussian war of 1870 and Otto von Bismarck's siege of Paris, two businessmen made a private vow to God to build a church if France was spared destruction. The building was consecrated in 1919, when a victorious France emerged from World War I, another war with Germany. To reach it, walk up the many steps, take the *funiculaire*, or wind your way up rue Ronsard, rue Maurice-Utrillo, and onto the square of the basilica, the *parvis*. The church is full of wonderful mosaics, statues, relief sculptures, and stained glass. The fabulous architecture is capped by the famous ovoid dome, the second highest point in Paris after the Eiffel Tower.

West of the basilica is the **Place du Tertre (6)** *(18th)*, full of quick-draw portraitists and swamped with tourists. Another Montmartre legend is that the term "bistro" originated here in the early 1800s when Russian soldiers in the restaurant **La Mère Catherine** shouted "Bistro!" ("Quickly!") for faster service. Northward, the cabaret **Au Lapin Agile (7)** *(22 rue des Saules, 18th, 01-46.06.85.87, www.au-lapin-agile.com; hours: Tu–Su 9PM–2AM)* retains its early 20th-century atmosphere when it was a favorite of artists and poets. Of the old village windmills, two remain, both in rue Lepic: Moulin du Radet (further down) and **Moulin de la Galette (8)** *(rue Lepic, 18th)*, which became a

dancehall that inspired work by Vincent van Gogh and Auguste Renoir. Many painters lived and had studios in tranquil **Avenue Junot (9)** *(18th)*. Nearby on a lovely square, **Le Bateau-Lavoir (10)** *(13 pl. Emile-Goudeau, 18th; closed to public)* was a neglected, run-down building of artists' studios and apartments shared in the early 1900s by Modigliani, Picasso, Braque, Juan Gris, and Marie Laurencin, among others. Here, in 1907, Picasso painted *Les Demoiselles d'Avignon*, considered the painting that launched Cubism. Now rebuilt, this historical building again provides studio and living space for emerging artists.

Arts & Entertainment:

The **Max Fourny Museum of Naïf Art (11)** *(Halle St-Pierre, 2 rue Ronsard, 18th, 01-42.58.72.89, www.hallesaint pierre.org; hours: M–F 10AM–6PM, Sa 10AM–7PM, Su 11AM–6PM; Aug M–F 12PM–6PM)* contains paintings and sculptures from more than 30 countries. Near the Place du Tertre, the **Espace Montmartre Salvador Dali (12)** *(11 rue Poulbot, 18th, 01-42.64.40.10, www.daliparis. com; hours: daily 10AM–6PM, Jul & Aug daily 10AM–8PM)* exhibits the Surrealist artist's work. The **Musée de Montmartre (13)** *(12 rue Cortot, 18th, 01-49.25.89.37, www.museedemontmartre.fr; hours: daily 10AM–6PM)* covers the history of Montmartre and its bohemian life, and includes a reconstruction of the Café de l'Abreuvoir, Utrillo's favorite café.

The art cinema **Studio 28 (14)** *(10 rue Tholozé, 18th, 01-46.06.36.07, www.cinemastudio28.com; call for show* *times or check Web site)* was decorated by Jean Cocteau. The **Théâtre de l'Atelier (15)** *(1 pl. Charles-Dullin, 18th, 01-46.06.49.24, www.theatre-atelier.com; call for show times or check Web site)* stages contemporary plays, both French and international.

PLACES TO EAT & DRINK
Where to Eat:

In an area that's a known tourist trap, a few restaurants offer good food at reasonable prices. A bread shop over a century ago, **L'Été en Pente Douce (16)** *(€-€€) (8 rue Paul-Albert, 18th, 01-42.64.02.67, www.parisresto.com; hours: daily 12PM–1AM)* is a most refreshing place for a lovely quiche or an afternoon tea, especially on the terrace facing the Butte Montmartre. **Le Moulin de la Galette (17)** *(€€-€€€) (83 rue Lepic, 18th, 01-46.06.84.77, www.lemoulindelagalette.fr; hours: daily 12PM–11PM)*, by the famous windmill, is a stunning, romantic locale with delectable food. A trendy, artistic Montmartre crowd converges on **Le Soleil Gourmand (18)** *(€-€€) (10 rue Ravignan, 18th, 01-42.51.00.50; hours: daily 12:30PM–2:30PM, 7:30PM–11PM)*: the food is simple; the ambience outstanding. Also super-hip is **Café Burq (19)** *(€€) (6 rue Burq, 18th, 01-42.52.81.27; hours: M–Sa 8PM–12AM)*, with terrific New French bistro fare, a great atmosphere, and music to match.

A talented Basque chef with culinary inspiration from Southeast Asia, Latin America, North Africa, and France has a hit on his hands: **La Famille (20)** *(€€) (41 rue des Trois-Frères, 18th, 01-42.52.11.12, restaurantlafamille.fr;*

hours: Tu–Sa 8PM–11PM) is one of the trendiest Parisian restaurants. The atmosphere is relaxed with a friendly and cool crowd, and good music to boot. Cheap, cheap, cheap: **L'Annexe (21) (€-€€)** *(13 rue des Trois-Frères, 18th, 01-46.06.12.48, www.lannexe-montmartre.fr; hours: M–Th 7PM–11PM, F–Sa 7PM–11:30PM)* isn't haute anything; it's simple, good, inexpensive food that comes in large portions. **L'Entracte (22) (€€)** *(44 rue d'Orsel, 18th, 01-46.06.93.41; hours: W–Sa 12PM–2PM, 7PM–10:30PM, Su 12PM–2PM)*, a tiny, intimate bistro, does classic French dishes very well.

Bars & Nightlife:

For songs of the good old days, the cabaret **Au Lapin Agile (7)** *(see also page 171)* has just the right touch of nostalgia. **La Bascule (23)** *(24 rue Durantin, 18th, 01-42.54.88.08; hours: M–Sa 4PM–2AM, Su 12PM–11PM)*, a wine bar with tapas, has a warm atmosphere and a decor bathed in red with Spanish influences and interesting moldings. It's a hit with the thirty-something crowd.

WHERE TO SHOP

Modern designs in glass, ceramics, and lighting are fabulous at **Pages 50/70: Olivier Verlet (24)** *(15 rue Yvonne-le-Tac, 18th, 01-42.52.48.59; hours: Tu–Sa 2PM–7PM, Su–M by appt)*.

Rue d'Orsel is full of wonderful boutiques, such as **Zelia sur la Terre comme au Ciel (25)** *(47 ter, rue d'Orsel, 18th, 01-46.06.96.51, www.zelia.net; by appt only)*, an extravagant, imaginative wedding shop. Look for high-design furniture and objects at **Galerie Christine Diegoni (26)**

(47 ter, rue d'Orsel, 18th, 01-42.64.69.48, www. christinediegoni.fr; hours: M–Sa 2PM–7PM). **Belle de Jour (27)** *(7 rue Tardieu, 18th, 01-46.06.15.28, www.belle-de-jour.fr; hours: Tu–F 10:30AM–1PM, 2PM–7PM, Sa 10:30AM–1PM, 2PM–6PM)* has every imaginable crystal perfume bottle.

Marché St-Pierre (28) *(2 rue Charles-Nodier, pl. St-Pierre, 18th, 01-46.06.92.25, www.marchesaintpierre.com; hours: M–F 10AM–6:30PM, Sa 10AM–7PM)* is the place to go for fabrics and trimmings; many shops offer discounted remnants. Emerging designers favor **rue des Gardes**. Beautifully lined, bright leather bags by **Luc Dognin (29)** *(4 rue des Gardes, 18th, 01-44.92.32.16, www.dognin paris.com)* are the rage all over Paris. **Lily Latifi (30)** *(11 rue des Gardes, 18th, 01-42.23.30.86, www.lilylatifi.com; hours: Th–Sa 2PM–7PM, M–W by appt)* meshes industrial design with applied and visual arts to create unusual fabrics that she turns into objects, clothing, and bags.

WHERE TO STAY

Exhibitions by local artists and magnificent views are some of the highlights of the formal but not pretentious **Terrass Hôtel (31)** (€€-€€€) *(12 rue Joseph-de-Maistre, 18th, 01-46.06.72.85, www.terrass-hotel.com)*. You get value for money at the quiet, clean, family-run **Hôtel des Arts (32)** (€-€€) *(5 rue Tholozé, 18th, 01-46.06.30.52, www.arts-hotel-paris.com)*. It's quite an uphill hike from the Métro, but the views are spectacular at the romantic, antique-filled **Ermitage Hôtel (33)** (€) *(24 rue Lamarck, 18th, 01-42.64.79.22, www.ermitagesacrecoeur.fr)*.

PIGALLE

❷ ⑫ *to Pigalle;* ❷ *to Blanche or Anvers*

● **SNAPSHOT** ●

Pigalle, once the sleazy red-light center of Paris, has begun cleaning up its neighborhood of streetwalkers, peep shows, and erotic cabarets. That cabaret scene was immortalized in the posters that Toulouse-Lautrec made of characters and places in Pigalle. His renderings of *danseuse* Jane Avril at dance halls such as the Moulin Rouge, the Divan Japonais, and Le Chat Noir, as well as his posters of *chansonnier* Aristide Bruant added atmosphere to the seediness of the quarter renowned for its brothels.

PLACES TO SEE
Landmarks:

Famous artists and infamous characters are buried in **Montmartre Cemetery (34)** *(20 ave. Rachel, 18th, 01-53.42.36.30; hours: Mar 16–Nov 5, M–Sa 7:30AM–6PM, Su 9AM–6PM; Nov 6–Mar 15 M–Sa 8:30AM–5PM, Su 9AM–5PM)*: dancer Nijinsky, filmmaker Truffaut, painter Degas, composers Berlioz and Offenbach, and writers Stendhal and Dumas *fils* lie beside La Goulue (Louise Weber, the first can-can performer and Toulouse-Lautrec's model), Alphonsine Plessis (consumptive inspi-

76

ration for Dumas's *La Dame aux Camélias*), and famed beauty Madame de Récamier.

The **Moulin Rouge (35)** *(82 bd. de Clichy, 18th, 01-53.09.82.82, www.moulin rouge.fr; show times daily: 9PM, 11PM; matinees 2:45PM)* was once a bawdy, populist cabaret theater. Today, while they still do the can-can there, it holds none of the original naughty atmosphere but is instead an expensive, Las Vegas-style tourist trap.

Arts & Entertainment:

In keeping with its location among the sex shops and shows of Pigalle, the **Museum of Eroticism (36)** *(72 bd. de Clichy, 18th, 01-42.58.28.73, www.musee-erotisme.com; hours: daily 10AM–2AM)* focuses on sex as a motif of folk art. On display are phalluses, fertility symbols, figurines, pictures, and a history of Parisian brothels. Instructive and funny, at times seedy, it's not erotic in itself.

PLACES TO EAT & DRINK
Where to Eat:

Basic food, a great wine list with artisan vintners, and a friendly atmosphere are what **L'Homme Tranquille (37)** *(€–€€) (81 rue des Martyrs, 18th, 01-42.54.56.28; hours: Tu–Sa 7:30PM–11:30PM)* offers. Locals know that **Chez Toinette (38)** *(€–€€) (20 rue Germain Pilon, 18th, 01-42.54.44.36, www.cheztoinette.com; hours: M–Sa from 7:30PM, closed Aug)* is a good deal: the young, arty clientele loves the fun, casual atmosphere and fills up on French home cooking. **Rose Bakery (39) (€)** *(46 rue des Martyrs, 9th, 01-42.82.12.80; hours: Tu–Su 9AM–7PM, closed 2 wks Aug)* has all things English but is especially good for tea and dessert.

Bars & Nightlife:

Though the Moulin Rouge (35) *(see also page 177)* has become a cheesy venue catering to tourists, other cabarets have turned into hip clubs. **Rue des Martyrs** is a happening spot. Toulouse-Lautrec's Le Divan Japonais has become **Le Divan du Monde (40)** *(75 rue des Martyrs, 18th, 01-40.05.06.99, www.ledivandumonde.com; hours vary)*, featuring a wide range of music, from hip-hop to Cuban, reggae to techno-pop, in a laid-back setting. At night the hip **La Fourmi (41)** *(74 rue des Martyrs, 18th, 01-42.64.70.35; hours: M–Th, 8AM–2AM, F–Sa 8AM–4AM, Su 10AM–1:30AM)* attracts both party-till-dawners and casual drinkers, goths, and the flannel-shirted set.

WHERE TO SHOP

Cutting-edge design characterizes **rue des Martyrs**. Vintage French 1950s-1970s objects and furnishings make Et puis c'est tout (42) *(72 rue des Martyrs, 9th, 01-40.23.94.02; hours: M 2PM–7PM, Tu–Sa 12PM–7:30PM)* stand out. Small, precious, a gem, a strand of gold–the stylish jewelry of Emmanuelle Zysman (43) *(81 rue des Martyrs, 18th, 01-42.52.01.00, www.emmanuelle zysman.fr; hours: Tu–F 11AM–2PM, 3PM–7PM, Sa 11AM–7PM)* is sold around the world. Elegant and simple, in gold with precious and semi-precious stones, her jewelry designs attract because of their purity and plain elegance. Hip young designers showcase their creations in rue des Martyrs, so stroll down the street and absorb the creators' efforts. Simple, unique, and beautiful, Patricia Louisor (44) *(16 rue Houdon, 18th, 01-42.62.10.42; hours: daily 12PM–8PM)* clothes are "for working, dancing, or seduction."

WHERE TO STAY

Paris Vacation Apartments (45) (€-€€€) *(86 bd. de Clichy, 18th, 06-42.00.82.07, 06-63.60.67.14 or 06-12.44.64.78, www.parisvacationapartments.com)* offer studios and apartments on a weekly rental basis to make you feel at home while taking in the city sights.

chapter 8

OUTSKIRTS OF PARIS

OUTSKIRTS OF PARIS

Places to See:

1. Bois de Boulogne
2. Parc André Citroën
3. Bois de Vincennes
4. Père Lachaise Cemetery
5. Belleville/Ménilmontant
6. Parc des Buttes-Chaumont
7. Parc de la Villette: City of Science; City of Music
8. Flea Market of St-Ouen
9. La Grande Arche de la Défense

> I could spend my whole life
> watching the Seine flow by…
> It is a poem of Paris.

—Blaise Cendrars

OUTSKIRTS OF PARIS

At the farther reaches of Paris are a number of notable spots that make for a lovely few hours or even a whole day. Although exploring these areas is recommended, it is not advisable to walk around the parks at night. These areas are at some distance from the main attractions of the city, so it is preferable to find a hotel in central Paris rather than in such outlying spots.

BOIS DE BOULOGNE (1) *(16th)*

2 *to Porte Dauphine;* **1** *to Porte Maillot or Les Sablons;* **10** *to Porte d'Auteuil*

West of Paris is the **Bois de Boulogne**, a stunning park of more than 2,000 acres. Once the royal hunting grounds, it is a magical forest with gardens, woods, lakes, châteaux, and racetracks, an idyllic place for walking, boating, bicycling, and other outdoor recreation. To tour the vast grounds, rent a bicycle near **Pavillon Royal** *(rte. de Suresnes)*, a short walk from the Art Nouveau Métro station **Porte Dauphine** *(M: 2)*. Among

the features of the Bois are the **Jardin d'Acclimatation** *(01-40.67.90.85, www.jardindacclimatation.fr, hours: Apr–Sep daily 10AM–7PM; Oct–Mar daily 10AM–6PM)*, a children's amusement park; the **Parc de Bagatelle** *(rte. de Sèvres à Neuilly)*, a park and château; and the romantic garden **Pré Catelan**, site also of a famous restaurant. The **Shakespeare Garden** contains flowers, trees, and plants that appear in the poet's plays, as well as an open-air theater. Two lakes, **Lac Supérieur** and **Lac Inférieur**, offer boating opportunities. France's two most famous horseracing tracks, **Hippodrome de Longchamp** (*rte. des Tribunes, 16th, 01-44.30.75.00, www. france-galop.com; call for race times or check Web site*) and **Hippodrome d'Auteuil** (*rte. d'Auteuil aux Lacs, 16th, 01-40.71.47.47, www.france-galop.com; call for race times or check Web site*), are located in the Bois. The **Stade Roland-Garros** (*Porte des Mousquetaires, 2 ave. Gordon-Bennett, 16th, 01-47.43.48.00, or book tours at 01-47.43.48.48, www.rolandgarros.com; museum: 01-47.43.48.48, www.fft.fr/roland-garros/musee; museum hours: W, F–Su 10AM–6PM*) hosts the annual French Open Tennis Championships (*late May–early Jun*). Kings kept their mistresses in châteaux in the Bois de Boulogne, giving the park its reputation for love; today, night brings out swingers of all sorts.

The French gastronomic treasure **Le Pré Catelan** (€€€€) (*rte. de Suresnes, 16th, 01-44.14.41.14, www.precatelan paris.com; hours: M–Sa 12PM–2:30PM, 7PM–10PM, book ahead*) serves exquisite French cuisine in a romantic setting. There are numerous restaurants (mostly elegant and expensive) and cafés in the park. A boat ride and enchanting outdoor setting enhance the dining experience at **Le Chalet des Iles** (€€) (*on the larger island of Lac Inférieur, Porte de la Muette, 16th, 01-42.88.04.69, www.chalet-des-iles.com; hours: daily 12PM–2PM, 7:30PM–9:30PM*).

PARC ANDRÉ CITROËN (2) *(15th)*

8 *to Balard;* **10** *to Javel/André-Citroën*

Parc André Citroën *(Quai André-Citroën)*, built on the grounds of the old Citroën car factory, is a marvel of landscape architecture. Greenhouses, ponds, fountains, gardens, and inventive formations of hedges and trees blend into a wonderland of primitive and formal nature.

BOIS DE VINCENNES (3) *(12th)*

1 *to Château de Vincennes;*
8 *to Porte de Charenton or Porte Dorée*

Like the Bois de Boulogne, the **Bois de Vincennes** *(www.paris.fr)* was once a royal hunting ground. On the southeast edge of Paris, it is home to a famous zoo, a floral garden, racetrack, château and fortress, and various sports and horticultural sites. Along the north side, the **Château de Vincennes** *(entry by the Tour du Village, 1 ave. de Paris, 12th, 01-48.08.31.20, http://en.chateau-vincennes.fr; hours: Sep 23–May 20 daily 10AM–5PM, May 21–Sep 22 daily 10AM–6PM)*, a medieval fortified castle, has been a royal residence, prison, porcelain factory, and arsenal. The castle keep is the château's museum. Nearby is **Parc Floral** *(rte. du Champ de Manoeuvre, 12th, 01-49.57.24.84, www.parcfloraldeparis.com; hours: daily 9:30AM–5/6/7/8PM, depending on season)*, a botanic

garden. The three lakes—**Lac des Minimes, Lac Daumesnil**, and **Lac de Gravelle**—are beautiful areas for walking and boating. In the **Parc Zoologique** (*53 ave. de St-Maurice, 12th, 01-44.75.20.00, www.mnhn.fr; closed for renovation til Apr 2014*) animals roam freely within large enclosures resembling their natural habitats. The Bois also houses the **Buddhist Temple of Paris** (*rte. de la Ceinture du Lac Daumesnil, 12th, 01-40.04.98.06, kagyu-dzong.org; office hours: Tu–Su 2PM–5PM, W 3PM–7PM*) and the **Aquarium of Tropical Fish** (*293 ave. Daumesnil, 12th, 01-53.59.58.60, www.aquarium-portedoree.fr; hours: Tu–F 10AM–5:30PM, Sa–Su 10AM–7PM*).

Deep within the Bois is the **Cartoucherie de Vincennes** (*rte. du Champ de Manoeuvre; from Métro Château de Vincennes, free shuttle bus, or bus 112*); once a munitions warehouse, it became home to some of the world's best avant-garde theater during the politically turbulent 1960s. Most famous of the five troupes housed there, the **Théâtre du Soleil** (*theatre 01-43.74.87.63, box office 01-43.74.24.08, www.theatre-du-soleil.fr; box office hours: daily 11AM–6PM*) is a must-see for anyone interested in theater. The troupe creates grand political epics using masks, puppets, and musicians, and drawing on international theater traditions. The other troupes are also inspiring: **Théâtre de l'Aquarium** (*01-43.74.99.61, box office 01-43.74.72.74, www.theatredelaquarium.net; box office hours: M 3PM–7PM, Tu–F 10AM–1PM, 2PM–7PM*); **Théâtre de la Tempête** (*01-43.28.36.36, www.la-tempete.fr; box office hours: Tu–F 11:30AM–1PM,*

2PM–6:30PM, Sa 2PM–6PM); **Théâtre de l'Épée de Bois** (01-48.08.18.75, box office 01-48.08.39.74, www. epeedebois.com; box office hours: Tu–Sa 10AM–7PM); and **Théâtre du Chaudron** (01-43.28.97.04, www.theatre duchaudron.fr; box office hours: M–F 2PM–6PM).

In the park there is a **café** (on **Reuilly Island** in Lac Daumesnil) and a **restaurant** (on **Porte Jaune Island** in Lac des Minimes). Theatrical productions at the **Cartoucherie** have the bonus of good food in the **lobby cafés**: the soup, bread, and sandwiches are homemade. A tiny treasure in a former butcher shop, **Les Zygomates** (€–€€) (7 rue de Capri, 12th, 01-40.19.93.04, www. leszygomates.fr; hours: Tu–Sa 12PM–2PM, 7:30PM– 10:30PM, closed Aug) serves excellent cuisine with a flair. Great Gascon food at the homey **Au Trou Gascon** (€€– €€€) (40 rue Taine, 12th, 01-43.44.34.26, www.autrou gascon.fr; hours: M–F 12PM–2PM, 7:30PM–10:30PM, closed Aug) includes foie gras and cassoulet.

Paris's most famous and most prestigious cemetery, **Père Lachaise** *(16 rue du Repos, main entrance at bd. de Ménilmontant, 20th, 01-55.25.82.10, www.pere-lachaise.com or www.pariscemeteries.com; hours: Mar 16–Nov 5 M–F 8AM–6PM, Sa 8:30AM–6PM, Su 9AM–6PM; Nov 6–Mar 15 M–F 8AM–5:30PM, Sa 8:30AM–5:30PM, Su 9AM–5:30PM)*, set on a wooded hill, is full of beautiful tombstones and funerary sculptures. Famous people interred here include Proust, Delacroix, Edith Piaf, Colette, Chopin, Balzac, Sarah Bernhardt, Oscar Wilde, Simone Signoret and Yves Montand, Alfred de Musset, Molière, La Fontaine, Abélard and Héloïse, Jim Morrison, Gertrude Stein and Alice B. Toklas, Richard Wright, Isadora Duncan, and Baron Haussmann.

The décor is run down, but the food and atmosphere at **Maison d'Italie** *(€-€€) (27 ave. Gambetta, 20th, 01-46.36.74.75; hours: daily 12PM–3PM, 6:30PM–11PM)* are delightful. The cozy, intimate West African restaurant **Waly Fay** *(€-€€) (6 rue Godefroy-Cavaignac, 11th, 01-40.24.17.79, www.walyfay.com, Metro: 9 to Charonne; hours: daily 7PM–2AM, closed Aug)* serves perfumed spicy stews and other delicacies in an elegant, warm ambience.

The retro music bar-café **Le Piston Pélican** *(15 rue de Bagnolet, 20th, 01-43.71.15.76, www.pistonpelican.com; hours: M–Sa 5PM–2AM, Su 2PM–11PM)*, with its atmospheric vintage bar and dining area resembling a train station waiting room, attracts a hip young crowd. In what was once a railway station, the trendy bar **La Flèche d'Or** *(102 bis, rue de Bagnolet, 20th, 01-44.64.01.02, www.flechedor.fr; call for hours & concert times)* gives free concerts on weeknights.

BELLEVILLE/MÉNILMONTANT (5) *(20th)*

② **⑪** *to Belleville;* **②** *to Couronnes or Ménilmontant;* **⑪** *to Pyrénées or Jourdain*

Belleville and **Ménilmontant**, the hilly area between Père Lachaise Cemetery and the Parc des Buttes-Chaumont, has seen a succession of some 60 different immigrant populations over the years, giving it a lively, diverse character. Edith Piaf, the torch singer who rose from poverty to international fame, was born at 72 rue de Belleville. Piaf memorabilia are gathered at the **Edith Piaf Museum** *(5 rue Crespin-du-Gast, 11th, 01-43.55.52.72; hours: by appt only M–W 1PM–6PM, Th 10AM–12PM).* Another famous neighborhood figure was singer and film star Maurice Chevalier. With artists and young Parisians increasingly claiming the turf, this fascinating quarter has gentrified significantly. Artists—painters, photographers, jewelers, musicians—open their studios to the public every year in mid-May at the **Portes Ouvertes** event, sponsored by the **AAB (Ateliers d'Artistes de Belleville)** *(1 rue Francis Picabia, 20th, 01-77.12.63.13, www.ateliers-artistes-belleville.org; hours: gallery M–F 4PM–8PM, Sa–Su 10AM–8PM; Portes Ouvertes artists' studios 2PM–9PM).* There are lots of funky bistros, cafés, and shops in the area.

A blast from the past, **Le Bistrot des Soupirs** (€€) *(49 rue de la Chine, 20th, 01-44.62.93.31, www.bistrot-des-soupirs.fr; hours: Tu–Th 12PM–2PM, 8PM–10PM, F–Sa 12PM–2PM, 8PM–11PM, closed last 2 wks Aug)* hasn't changed since the 1950s; the bistro fare and wines are classic. Refined contemporary bistro cuisine, Art Deco setting, and an animated ambience is what you get at **Le Zéphyr** (€€) *(1 rue Jourdain, 20th, 01-46.36.65.81; hours: bar daily 8AM–2AM; restaurant daily 12PM–3:30PM, 7:30PM–11:30PM)*. The wine bar **Le Baratin** (€-€€) *(3 rue Jouye-Rouve, 20th, 01-43.49.39.70; hours: Tu–F 12:15PM–3PM, 8PM–11PM, Sa 8PM–11PM, closed 3 wks Aug)* serves generous portions of hearty food along with unusual wines. For great Thai, don't miss **Lao Siam** (€-€€) *(49 rue de Belleville, 19th, 01-40.40.09.68; hours: M–Sa 12PM–2PM, 7PM–10PM, Su 12PM–2PM)*.

Alternative cool and streetwise urban chic reigns among young designers of **rue Oberkampf**, where the bar scene buzzes at night. It all started with **Café Charbon** *(109 rue Oberkampf, 11th, 01-43.57.55.13, www.lecafecharbon.com; hours: Su–W 9AM–2AM, Th–Sa 9AM–4AM)*, the cool and stylish Belle-Époque music bar-café, and its nightclub annex **Nouveau Casino** *(01-43.57.57.40, www.nouveaucasino.net; call for concert & club hours)*. Celebrities and locals love the trendy, arty bar **La Mère Lachaise** *(78 bd. de Ménilmontant, 20th, 01-47.97.61.60; hours: daily 9AM–2AM)*, with its fabulous terrace.

PARC DES BUTTES-CHAUMONT (6) (19th)

7 to Louis Blanc, then
7bis to Buttes Chaumont or Botzaris

Baron Haussmann converted a garbage dump and quarry on a hill into the **Parc des Buttes-Chaumont** (*rue Manin, main entrance at rue Armand Carrel, buttes chaumont.free.fr; hours: May 1–Sep 29 daily 7AM–10PM, Sep 30–Apr 30 daily 7AM–8PM*), located in a working-class neighborhood. A lake was created, with an island and footbridge, streams, a waterfall, and beaches. A Romanesque temple stands on the hilltop.

Located within the park, **Chez Vincent Cozzoli–Pavillon Puebla** (€€-€€€) (*Parc des Buttes-Chaumont, 19th; use park entrance at 3 ave. Simon-Bolivar, 01.42.02.22.45, vincentcozzoli.com; hours: M–Sa 8PM–2AM*) may be one of the best Italian restaurants in Paris. Chef Mehdi Corthier prepares fabulously imaginative new bistro fare at his restaurant **La Table de Botzaris** (€€-€€€) (*10 rue du Général-Brunet, 19th, 01-40.40.03.30, www.latable debotzaris.com; hours: Tu–Sa 12PM–2:30PM, 7PM–10:30PM, Su brunch 11:30AM–2:30PM*).

PARC DE LA VILLETTE: CITY OF SCIENCE; CITY OF MUSIC (7) *(19th)*

7 *to Porte de la Villette;* **5** *to Porte de Pantin*

Built on what was once the city's slaughterhouses and livestock market, the sprawling **Parc de la Villette** is home to an amazing complex of museums and exhibition halls. The **Cité des Sciences et de l'Industrie** *(30 ave. Corentin-Cariou, 19th, 01-40.05.70.00, www.citesciences.fr; hours: Tu–Sa 10AM–6PM, Su 10AM–7PM)* reveals the world of science and technology through multimedia exhibits, interactive displays, films, and conferences. The smaller **Cité de la Musique** *(221 ave. Jean-Jaurès, 19th, 01-44.84.44.84, www.citedelamusique.fr; hours: Tu–Sa 12PM–6PM, Su 10AM–6PM)* houses, among other things, a music conservatory and a museum of music.

Head to **Avenue Jean-Jaurès** for meals or drinks. True to the district's old slaughterhouse renown, **Au Boeuf Couronné** (€€-€€€) *(188 ave. Jean-Jaurès, 19th, 01-42.39.44.44, www.boeuf-couronne.com, www.gerard-joulie.com; hours: daily 12PM–3PM, 7PM–12AM)* serves great classic beef dishes. In turn-of-the-century décor, **Bistro 190** (€-€€) *(190 ave. Jean-Jaurès, 19th, 01-40.40.09.39; hours: daily 12PM–3PM, 7PM–11PM)* serves wonderful traditional cuisine. **Café de la Musique** (€-€€) *(213 ave. Jean-Jaurès, 19th, 01-48.03.15.91, www.citedelmusique.fr; hours: daily 8AM–2AM)* is a trendy café better for people-watching than meals.

FLEA MARKET OF ST-OUEN (8) *(18th)*

④ *to Porte de Clignancourt*

Extending across 15 acres, at the largest of Parisian flea markets, the **Marché aux Puces de St-Ouen** *(main artery: 140 rue des Rosiers, St-Ouen, just north of the 18th, 01-40.11.77.36, www.marcheauxpuces-saintouen.com; hours: Sa, 9AM–6PM, Su 10AM–6PM, M 11AM–5PM)*, some 2,500 dealers sell antiques, artwork, furniture, books, jewelry, and odds and ends.

LA GRANDE ARCHE DE LA DÉFENSE (9)
(NW border of Paris)

① *to La Défense/Grande Arche,*
Ⓐ *to La Défense/Grande Arche*

In 1981 President François Mitterand began a campaign to construct buildings with a cultural focus. Among the many creations that resulted from this project of *Grands Travaux* or "Great Works," some of the most spectacular are the Institute of the Arab World *(see Chapter 5, page 115)*, I. M. Pei's Louvre Pyramid *(see Chapter 2, page 50)*, the Opéra Bastille *(see Chapter 4, page 97)*, and the Grande Arche of La Défense.

La Défense is a large office building complex just beyond the northwestern edge of Paris. Built in the 1960s, its skyscrapers seemed to catapult French business into the supermodern era. Here, some of Europe's tallest buildings are the workplace of more than 100,000 people. Individually, the skyscrapers are unimpressive;

but taken as a whole, the development rivals business complexes in the U.S. and Asia. Into this expanse of mushrooming towers, a landmark was built in 1989 for the bicentennial of the French Revolution: the **Grande Arche** *(Paris La Défense, 01-49.07.27.27, www.grandearche.com; hours: Apr–Aug daily 10AM–8PM; Sep–Mar daily 10AM–7PM).* It is an enormous hollow cube under which the entire cathedral of Notre Dame could fit. Inside, there is an exhibition gallery and conference center; glass elevators whisk you heavenward to the roof for a spectacular view of Paris.

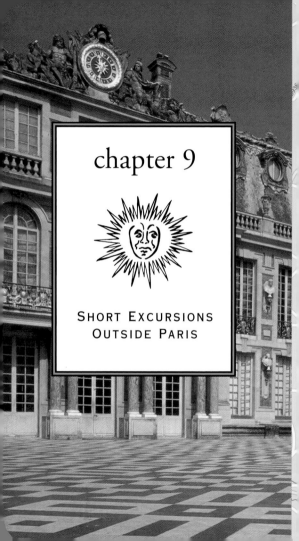

chapter 9

SHORT EXCURSIONS OUTSIDE PARIS

SHORT EXCURSIONS OUTSIDE PARIS

Places to See:

When I go out into the
countryside and see the sun and
the green and everything flowering,
I say to myself, "Yes indeed,
all that belongs to me!"

—*Henri Rousseau*

These areas of historic significance, cultural interest, and natural beauty can each be seen in a day trip. All have hotels for those preferring overnight stays.

VERSAILLES (1)

RER: *C5 to Versailles Rive-Gauche/Château de Versailles*
Or SNCF Train: *Gare St-Lazare station to Versailles Rive-Droite; Gare Montparnasse station to Versailles-Chantiers (average travel time: 30-45 minutes)*

Louis XIV, the "Sun King," made the palace of **Versailles** *(01-30.83.78.00; advance tickets at FNAC ticket offices and other outlets, see www.chateau versailles.fr; hours: Nov–Mar Tu–Su, château 9AM–5:30PM, estate 12PM–5:30PM, gardens daily 8AM–6PM; Apr–Oct Tu–Su, château 9AM–6:30PM, estate 12PM–6:30PM, gardens daily 8AM–8:30PM)* into the symbol of absolute monarchy. It remained the seat of royal political power from 1682 until the Revolution, a century later. The resplendent château, the largest in Europe, lodged 20,000 people at a time. Ornate and luxurious, it is surrounded by formal gardens with statues, canals, pools, and fountains. Louis XIV held extravagant parties and receptions here. He built a smaller palace, the **Grand Trianon**, for himself and his mistress.

Later, Louis XV built the **Petit Trianon**, his own retreat, which became Marie-Antoinette's favorite.

A good seafood restaurant is **La Marée de Versailles** (€€) *(22 rue au Pain, Versailles, 01-30.21.73.73, www. restaurantl-poisson-versailles.com; hours: Tu–Sa 12PM–2PM, 7:15PM–10PM, Su 12PM–2PM)*. Exquisite haute cuisine in an elegant ambience is a near-regal experience at **Gordon Ramsay au Trianon** (€€€€) *(Hôtel Trianon Palace, 1 bd. de la Reine, Versailles, 01-30.84.55.55, www.trianonpalace.com; hours: Tu–Th 7PM–10:30PM, F–Sa 12PM–2:30PM, 7PM–10:30PM, gallery area daily 10:30AM–1AM)*. For more info, restaurants, and accommodations, contact the **Versailles Tourist Office** *(Sofitel Building, 2 bis, ave. de Paris, 01-39.24.88.88, www. versailles-tourisme.com; hours: Apr–Oct M 10AM–6PM, Tu–Su 9AM–7PM; Nov–Mar Su–M 11AM–5PM, Tu–Sa 9AM–6PM)*.

CHARTRES (2)

SNCF Train: *Gare Montparnasse station to Chartres (average travel time: 1 hour)*

The magnificent Gothic cathedral of **Chartres** *(18 Cloître Notre Dame, cathedral 02-37.21.59.08, museum 02-37.21.22.07, www.cathedrale-chartres.org, www. chartres.fr, www.monuments-nationaux.fr; hours: daily cathedral 8:30AM–7:30PM, Jul–Aug Tu, F, Su 8:30AM–10PM; museum, call for hours)* is noted for its incredible stained-glass windows and its elaborately sculpted statues and reliefs. Behind the cathedral, the

Musée des Beaux-Arts (29 cloître Notre-Dame, 02-37.90.45.80, www.chartres.fr; hours: May–Oct W, Sa 10AM–12PM, 2PM–6PM; Su 2PM–6PM; Nov–Apr W, Sa 10AM–12PM, 2PM–5PM, Su 2PM–5PM) holds Renaissance paintings and tapestries. The **Maison de l'Archéologie** (2 rue au Lin, 02-37.23.42.20; call for hours) recounts the story of the excavation of a Gallo-Roman city. A path along the banks of the Eure River leads to the ruins of the old Roman city wall.

There are plenty of restaurants in town; **L'Estocade** (€-€€) (1 rue de la Porte-Guillaume, 02-37.34.27.17, www.estocade.net; hours: Tu–Su 12PM–2PM, 7:30PM–10PM) has a river view. For accommodations and other info, go to the **Chartres Tourist Office** (Maison Saumon, 8 rue de la Poissonnerie, 02-37.18.26.26, www.chartres-tourisme.com; hours: Apr 15–Oct 14 M–Sa 9:30AM–6:30PM, Su 10AM–5:30PM; Oct 15–Apr 14 M–Sa 10AM–6PM, Su 10AM–5PM).

GIVERNY (3)

SNCF Train: Gare St-Lazare station to Vernon, then 3-mile taxi ride or bus (average travel time: 1 hour)

Claude Monet lived in **Giverny** with his mistress and eight children and created his superb Impressionist paintings there. The famous water-lily pond, with its weeping willows and Japanese bridge, is a favorite spot. The house-museum, **Fondation Claude Monet** (84 rue de Claude Monet, 02-32.51.28.21, www.fondation-monet.fr; hours: Apr–Oct daily 9:30AM–6PM, come early), has no original Monets but plenty of memorabilia. Nearby, the **Musée Américain de Giverny** *(99 rue Claude Monet, 02-32.51.94.65, giverny.org/museums/american; hours: Apr–Oct daily 10AM–6PM)* is dedicated to American impressionists who worked in France in Monet's time.

The famous **Hôtel Baudy (€-€€)** *(81 rue Claude-Monet, 02-32.21.10.03, www.giverny.fr/restaurant-baudy; hours: Apr–Oct daily 10AM–9:30PM, reserve ahead)* is a museum-restaurant where some of Monet's American followers lived and worked. For overnight stays, **La Musardiere (€)** *(123 rue Claude Monet, 02-32.21.03.18, www.lamusardiere.fr)* is a lovely hotel dating back to 1880. It also features a restaurant with a terrace and garden. **Le Coin des Artistes (€)** *(65 rue Claude-Monet, 02-32.21.36.77, www.giverny.fr/le-coin-des-artistes)* is a B&B with an art gallery. For more info on Giverny, restaurants, and lodgings, go to *giverny.org*, or try the **Vernon Tourist Office** *(36 rue Carnot, in Vernon, 02-32.51.39.60, www.giverny-village.fr, www.vernon-visite.org; hours: May–Sep Tu–Sa 9AM–12:30PM, 2PM–6PM, Su 10AM–12PM; Oct–Apr Tu–Sa 9AM–12:30PM, 2PM–5:30PM)*.

SNCF Train: *Gare de Lyon station to Fontainebleau-Avon, then bus AB, marked "Château" (buy a "Forfait Château de Fontainebleau" ticket, which includes train and bus fare, château entrance fee, and audio guide) (average travel time: 1 hour)*

Though not as sprawling or magnificent as Versailles, the **Château de Fontainebleau** *(01-60.71.50.70, www.musee-chateau-fontainebleau.fr; hours: Apr–Sep W–M 9:30AM–6PM; Oct–Mar W–M 9:30AM–5PM)*, residence of French rulers, underwent transformations that give it a mix of styles. Napoleon I built an ornate throne room and his own extravagant quarters in the palace. Explore the wonderful gardens and forest.

Rue Grande is dotted with restaurants. Try the creative cuisine at **Au Délice Impérial** *(€-€€) (1 rue Grande, 01-64.22.20.70; hours: daily 7AM–1AM)*. Modern furniture and flooring juxtaposed with the 17th-century wine cellar setting at **Le Caveau des Lys** *(€€-€€€) (24 rue de Ferrare, 01-64.24.60.56; hours: Tu–Su 12PM–2PM, 7:15PM–10PM)* to create an unusual ambience. The friendly staff serve superb traditional French cuisine. **Hôtel Aigle Noir** *(€€) (27 pl. Napoléon-Bonaparte, 01-60.74.60.00, www.hotelaiglenoir.fr)*, built in the 15th century, sits across from the Fontainebleau castle gardens. You'll feel at home in its warm, elegant rooms. Elegant **Hôtel Napoléon** *(€-€€) (9 rue Grande, 01-60.39.50.50, www.hotelnapoleon-fontainebleau.com)* is footsteps away from the château and provides a refined and charming setting. For info and maps, as well as bike rentals, go to the **Fontainebleau Area Tourist Office** *(4 rue Royale, 01-60.74.99.99, www.fontainebleau-tourisme.com; hours: May–Oct M–Sa 10AM–6PM; Su 10AM–1PM, 2PM–5PM; Nov–May M–Sa 10AM–6PM, Su 10AM–1PM).*

MALMAISON (5)

RER: *A1 to La Défense, then bus 258 (travel time varies depending on your starting point in Paris)*

Napoleon and Josephine's love-nest **Malmaison** *(ave. du Château, 92500 Rueil-Malmaison, 01-41.29.05.55, www.chateau-malmaison.fr or www.napoleon.org; hours: Apr–Sep M, W–F 10AM–12:30PM, 1:30PM–5:45PM, Sa–Su 10AM–12:30PM, 1:30PM–6:15PM; Oct–Mar M, W–F 10AM–12:30PM, 1:30PM–5:15PM, Sa–Su 10AM–12:30PM, 1:30PM–5:45PM)* became her home after the divorce. The museum is dedicated to Napoleon and the First Empire. Don't miss Josephine's famous rose garden.

CHANTILLY (6)

SNCF Train: *Gare du Nord station to Chantilly-Gouvieux (average travel time: 30 minutes on train, plus 5-minute walk to town, 20-minute walk to château)*

Chantilly, domain of the Condé Princes, is known for its lace, for the invention of Chantilly whipped cream, and for its equestrian history of prestigious horseraces and hunting forests. The fairy tale **castle of Chantilly**, with

its parks and incredible stables, houses the **Condé Museum** *(03-44.27.31.80, www.chateaudechantilly.com; hours: Apr–Oct W–M 10AM–6PM, Nov–Mar W–M 10:30AM–5PM)*, with works by Raphael, Botticelli, Giotto, and Holbein. The **Musée Vivant du Cheval** *(Les Grandes Écuries, 03-44.27.31.80, www.museevivant ducheval.fr; call for hours)*, in the Grandes Écuries stables, shows horses and gives riding displays (first Sunday of every month). Every June, high society descends on the Chantilly racecourse for the flat-racing trophies, a prestigious and fashionable event.

The tea room in the hamlet of the castle, **Aux Goûters Champêtres** *(€-€€)* *(03-44.57.46.21; call for hours)*, features the famous whipped cream. On Chantilly's main street, the cozy bistro **Le Goutillon** *(€-€€)* *(61 rue du Connétable, 03-44.58.01.00)* offers home-style cooking. For info, restaurants, and lodgings, contact the **Chantilly Tourist Office** *(60 ave. Maréchal-Joffre, 03-44.67.37.37, www.chantilly-tourisme.com; hours: May-Sep M–Sa 9:30AM–12:30PM, 1:30PM–5:30PM, Su 10AM–1:30PM; Oct–Apr M–Sa 9:30AM–12:30PM, 1:30PM–5:30PM)*, near the station.

SNCF Train: *Gare de l'Est station to Reims (average travel time: 90 minutes)*

Most French monarchs were crowned in Reims. **Notre-Dame de Reims** *(3 rue Guillaume de Machault, 03-26.47.55.34, www.cathedrale-reims.com; hours: daily 7:30AM–7:30PM)* is an ornately decorated Gothic cathedral with many beautiful stained-glass windows, including some of Chagall's designs.  Located in the region of Champagne, the area is home to France's finest bubbly. For general information, go to *www.maisons-champagne.com.* Visits to champagne houses are by appointment only: **Pommery** *(5 pl. du Général Gouraud, 03-26.61.62.56, www.pommery.com; hours: Apr–Oct daily 10AM–6PM; Nov–Mar daily 10AM–5PM),* **Krug** *(5 rue Coquebert, 03-26.84.44.20, www.krug.com),* **Veuve Clicquot** *(1 pl. des Droits-de-l'Homme, 03-26.89.53.90, www.veuve-clicquot.com; hours: by appt only Apr–Oct Tu–Sa 10AM–12:30PM, 1:30PM–6PM, Nov–Mar Tu–F 10AM–12:30PM, 1:30–6PM, closed mid-Dec to mid-Feb),* **Lanson** *(66 rue de Courlancy, 03-26.78.50.50, www.lanson.com; hours: by appt only M–F, closed Aug),* and **Roederer** *(21 bd. Lundy, 03-26.40.42.11, www.champagne-roederer.com; hours: by appt & recommendation).* At **Épernay** (18 miles away), **Moët et Chandon** *(20 ave. de Champagne, Épernay, 03-26.51.20.20, www.moet.com; tour hours: Apr–mid-Nov daily 9:30AM–11:30AM,*

2PM–4:30PM; Feb–Mar & mid-Nov–Dec M–F 9:30AM–11:30AM, 2PM–4:30PM; closed Jan; boutique: Apr–mid-Nov daily 9:30AM–5:30PM, mid-Nov–Dec & Feb–Mar M–F 9:30AM–1PM, 2PM–5:30PM) and **Mercier** *(68 ave. de Champagne, Épernay, 03-26.51.22.22, www.champagnemercier.fr; hours: call or see Web site for wine cellar visiting hours; appts necessary only for groups of 10 or more)* do great tours.

You can find many cafés and brasseries on **Place Drouet d'Erlon** that serve good meals. Try **Aux Coteaux** *(€-€€)* *(86-88 pl. Drouet d'Erlon, 03-26.47.08.79, www. auxcoteaux.com; hours: Tu–Sa 11:45AM–2PM, 6:30PM–11:45PM)* for tasty pizza and other delicious dishes. For more info, contact the **Reims Tourist Office** *(2 rue Guillaume de Machault, 08-92.70.13.51, www. reims-tourisme.com; hours: Oct–Mar M–Sa 9AM–6PM, Su 10AM–4PM; Apr–Sep M–Sa 9AM–7PM, Su 10AM–6PM)*. In the town of **Épernay**, **La Cave à Champagne** *(€-€€)* *(16 rue Gambetta, Épernay, 03-26.55.50.70, www.la-cave-a-champagne.com; hours: Th–M 12PM–2PM, 7PM–10PM, Tu 12PM–2PM)* is a good classic bistro. And if you get full from your meal, and fancy an overnight stay, the **Hôtel de Champagne** *(€)* *(30 rue Eugène-Mercier, Épernay, 03-26.53.10.60, www.bw-hotel-champagne.com)* is a comfortable hotel chain.

THEME PARKS:
MICKEY AND ASTÉRIX

DISNEYLAND PARIS (8)
RER: *A4 to Marne-la-Vallée/Chessy.*
(One-day RER + Disneyland Paris tickets
sold at major Métro stations.)

Disneyland Paris *(Marne-la-Vallée, 01-60.30.50.70, 08-25.30.60.30, www.disneylandparis.com; call for hours or check Web site)* has all the usual Disney fun.

PARC ASTÉRIX (9)
RER: *B3 to Roissy/Aéroport Charles-de-Gaulle 1,*
then shuttle bus (platform A3)

At Parc Astérix *(60128 Plailly, 03-44.62.31.31, 08-26.30.10.40, www. parcasterix.fr; call for hours or check Web site),* the Gauls compete with Disney.

NOTES

NOTES

PETER PAUPER PRESS
Fine Books and Gifts Since 1928

Our Company

In 1928, at the age of twenty-two, Peter Beilenson began printing books on a small press in the basement of his parents' home in Larchmont, New York. Peter—and later his wife, Edna—sought to create fine books that sold at "prices even a pauper could afford."

Today, still family owned and operated, Peter Pauper Press continues to honor our founders' legacy—and our customers' expectations—of beauty, quality, and value.

Métro &
RER map